THE
FINE ART
OF
GETTING
ALONG
WITH
OTHERS

By Dale Galloway

Rebuild Your Life
Twelve Ways to Develop a Positive Attitude
Expect a Miracle
You Can Win with Love
How to Feel Like a Somebody
Dare to Discipline Yourself
The Fine Art of Getting Along with Others

THE
FINE ART
OF
GETTING
ALONG
WITH
OTHERS

DALE E. GALLOWAY

© 1984 by Dale Galloway

Published by Revell
a division of Baker Publishing Group
PO Box 6287, Grand Rapids, MI 49516-6287
www.revellbooks.com

Spire edition published 2021

ISBN 978-0-8007-4044-3

Previously published by the Fleming H. Revell Company in 1984

Printed in the United States of America

Unless otherwise indicated, Scripture quotations are from the King James Version of the Bible.

Scripture quotations labeled AP are the author's paraphrase.

Scripture quotations labeled NEB are from The New English Bible. Copyright © The Delegates of the Oxford University Press and the Syndics of the Cambridge University Press 1961, 1970. Reprinted by permission.

Scripture quotations labeled NIV are taken from the HOLY BIBLE NEW INTERNATIONAL VERSION, copyright © 1978, by the New York International Bible Society. Used by permission of Zondervan Bible Publishers.

Scripture quotations labeled RSV are from the Revised Standard Version of the Bible, copyrighted 1946, 1952, © 1971 and 1973.

Scripture quotations labeled TLB are from The Living Bible, Copyright © 1971 by Tyndale House Publishers, Wheaton, Ill. Used by permission.

Quotation from Rebuild Your Life by Dale E. Galloway, published by Tyndale House Publishers, Inc., © 1975 by Dale E. Galloway. Used by permission.

Material from Say It with Love by Howard Hendricks, published by Victor Books.

"Love Will Bring Us Together—Because" taken from You Can Win with Love by Dale Galloway, copyright 1976 Harvest House Publishers, 1075 Arrowsmith, Eugene, Oregon 97402. Used by permission.

Baker Publishing Group publications use paper produced from sustainable forestry practices and post-consumer waste whenever possible.

21 22 23 24 25 26 27   7 6 5 4 3 2 1

Contents

5

Introduction

The "Secret" of Getting Along with Others

Five ways to begin to apply the secret

A middle-aged man visited my office to proclaim to me and my church that his was a normal, morally acceptable lifestyle.

How difficult I found it to listen to this man whose views ran counter to all I believe! Yet as I remained open to him, in love, he began to tell me his story. Out poured the pain of an anguish-laden life. Hurt filled his eyes as he shared, "I would give anything to have meaningful, lasting relationships in my life."

From that encounter I've learned that most of us echo that cry, no matter what our lifestyle. How few persons feel satisfied that their relationships could fit this positive description.

As Christians, we are tempted to believe ourselves exempt from such problems. But after being brought up in a church administrator's home, attending a Christian college and seminary, and pastoring for twenty years, I can testify that this is not true.

The past three months have shown me a pastor and his wife who have separated, admitting that they've never gotten along the entire time they've been married; a brilliant professional man who has quit his job because he could not get along with his boss; a nearby church that has split because the board and pastor could not agree. Christians were involved in all these situations, and we have all faced similar problems at home, at work, or with friends. Obviously, otherwise mature Christians may still remain deficient in the all-important area of getting along with other people.

For most people getting along is a matter of degree. Imagine rating your ability to get along with other people on a scale from one to ten. Few would be at either extreme of the scale. For most of us, it is not a matter of either getting along with everyone or with no one. Some people we get along with well, and other people we don't. I am going to reveal a secret to you. When you know it and put it to work in your life, it will immediately raise your level on the scale. When that happens, your relationships are going to be improved and much more enjoyable.

How Do I Get In on the Secret?

Jesus, the wisest, most knowledgeable person on the art of human relationships, gave us this Golden Rule principle:

• Principle 1 •

"Treat others as you want to be treated."

See Luke 6:31

You want to get along well with other people? Then put yourself in their place and try to understand them. You want people to like you? Then treat them as you would like to be treated if you were in their place.

In seeking to apply this great principle, I asked myself, *How would I really like to be treated*? After much thought, I have identified five ways I want to be treated in my roles as a pastor, counselor, husband, and friend.

- I want to be valued as a person of worth.
- I want to be listened to by other people.
- I want to be appreciated.
- I want to be built up and edified by others.
- I want to be treated with empathy.

I believe I am not unique in how I want to be treated. Others, even little children, have the same need for good treatment.

Five Ways People Would Like to Be Treated

1. People Want to Feel They Are of Worth. In 1960 I had just graduated from Olivet Nazarene College. That summer, while waiting to enter seminary in the fall, I pastored a struggling little church in a suburb of Chicago.

One day I went to one of the better known hospitals in Chicago to visit a patient. While there I ran into the chief of surgeons, Dr. Howard Hamlin, who for years had been a personal friend of my father and mother. As Dr. Hamlin and I walked down the hall together, an incident happened that was a little thing to the doctor but made a lasting impression on my life.

I remember feeling like a very important person walking alongside this important man. Not only was he a pacesetter in surgery at a major hospital in one of the biggest cities in the world, but he was a well-known lay leader in our denomination. We were walking along chitchatting when it happened.

Dr. Hamlin stopped and engaged the elderly hospital maintenance man in conversation. Calling the man by his first name, he proceeded to ask personal questions about the man's children. With a beaming face the man responded to the doctor's personal interest and shared those concerns closest to his heart.

Here was a busy doctor, one of my idols, stopping to talk to this man as if he were the most important person in the whole world.

When the conversation ended and we continued on down the hall, I looked back. The man was smiling, whistling, and mopping the floor as if he had the most important job in the hospital. Dr. Hamlin had given him the priceless gift of worth and dignity. Come to think of it, I felt pretty special myself that day, walking beside the considerate and kind doctor.

Dr. Hamlin practiced the key principle in human relationships by treating others as he wanted to be treated. In doing so, he was following in the steps of the Master, for Jesus never met an unimportant person. He met people from every level of society and treated them as special persons.

Jesus taught that we should do likewise: "Inasmuch as ye have done it unto one of the least of these my brethren, ye have done it unto me" (Matt. 25:40). The way we treat others is the way we are treating Jesus. We should treat them the same special way we would treat Him.

2. People Want to Be Listened To. "The road to the heart," wrote Voltaire, "is the ear." We've all had the experience of talking and suddenly realizing that those to whom we are speaking aren't listening. It is a downright deflating experience. On the other hand, when someone listens to me attentively, with good eye contact and interested response, it makes me feel good about myself and also gives me warm feelings toward that person.

If you want people to like you, all you have to do is start practicing the admonition: "Dear brothers, don't ever forget that it is best to listen much, speak little, and not become angry" (James 1:19 TLB). In other words, in a conversation stop worrying about what to say next and start really listening with an interested ear to what the other person says, and you will gain a friend.

3. People Want to Be Appreciated. After I spoke to a writer's guild, several people expressed their appreciation. Do you know what? I loved it. Dr. William James has said, "The deepest principle in human nature is the craving for appreciation." Mark Twain said he could live for three weeks on a compliment. Let's face it, I like to be appreciated. So do you. Everyone relishes receiving appreciation.

You do want to get along well with people, don't you? Then why not give them the words of praise and appreciation they crave? Do this, and people will love you for it.

4. People Want to Be Built Up and Edified. We live in a world of put-downs. You start building people up and edifying them, and you're going to stand head and shoulders above the crowd. Victor Hugo stated, "Man lives more by affirmation than by bread."

When you affirm someone by positive words, it creates a bond of goodwill and good feeling between you. Knowing this, you can use your tongue for good and not evil. The Bible says that the tongue has the power of life and death (see Prov. 18:21). It also teaches that evil words destroy but godly words will build up a person (see Prov. 11:9).

Howard Hendricks, in his book *Say It with Love*, tells his own true story:

> I can remember only two public school teachers I ever had, my fifth grade teacher and my sixth grade teacher. It kind of amuses me that I should be teaching, because school was just a bad-news item all the way for me. I could never get together with my school teachers on the basic objectives of the thing. The moment they would go out of the room I would go into action.
>
> Finally, my fifth grade teacher, Miss Simon, tied me to my seat, my hands behind my back, with a great big rope. Then she took mucilage paper and started over my mouth and went clear around my neck. "Now, Howard," she said, "you will sit still and keep quiet." So what else could I do?
>
> Finally I graduated from her class for obvious reasons, and I went on to my sixth grade teacher. I'll never forget her, Miss Noe, 6'4" tall—sort of a feminine version of Sherlock Holmes. I used to think that if that dear lady had done nothing but just stand erect, she would have done something for me.
>
> I walked into her class. The first thing she said was, "Oh, you're Howard Hendricks. I've heard a lot about you." Then she jarred me by adding, "But I don't believe a word of it." That year I found the first teacher who ever convinced me that she believed in me, and, you know, I never let that woman down. I would knock myself out for her. I would work and do all kinds of extra projects. My most vivid memories of that class are of occasionally looking over at the door with the little window pane

> The way to get along with other people is to stop looking at what's wrong with them and start seeing what they can become.
>
> To get along better with the people in your life, make a conscious effort to build them up.

in it and seeing Miss Simon, my fifth grade teacher, peeking in to see this thing which was come to pass. Here I was, sitting clothed in my right mind, and working.

Just think what this sixth-grade teacher who knew and practiced the secret of getting along did for this difficult child. By believing in him and treating him as she would want to be treated in his place, she became an instrument of God to get him turned around and headed on the right path. No wonder that after all these years she still stands out in seminary professor Dr. Howard Hendricks's mind as being the one teacher whom he fondly remembers.

5. People Want to Be Treated with Empathy. A cold wind howled, and the rain beat down when the telephone rang at a rural doctor's house. "It's my wife," the voice said. "She needs a doctor right away!"

"Can you come and get me?" asked the physician. "My car is being repaired."

"What?" came the sputtering reply. "Go out in this weather?"

How often we expect from others what we are unwilling to do ourselves, as this story shows. Frequently we have this attitude because we have not tried to put ourselves in another's place. We don't try to feel what he feels or see things from his viewpoint. Instead we become busy with our own thoughts, concentrate on making our own points, and worry about our own egos. As a result, we end up living in our own world, apart from others.

That is not God's way. The Bible teaches us to weep with those who weep and laugh with those who laugh (see Rom. 12:15). When we really do this, everything comes together. People feel listened to, appreciated, built up, and helped. Close relationships spring from the sharing of joys and sorrows. We begin to form right relationships through caring.

Someone has said, "The Kingdom of God is a kingdom of right relationships." You can become a partner with Christ in bringing His Kingdom of reconciliation to this earth. Right relationships result from this number-one principle: "Treat others as you want to be treated." People will not relate to you well unless you treat them right.

Did you ever stop to think why the members of the human race have so much trouble getting along with each other? Regardless of our race, creed, nationality, or sex, we all share this perplexing problem. The Bible teaches that its cause is that apart from the grace of God, man is by nature self-centered. And a selfish person thinks first, second, and most of the time not of others but of himself. That attitude destroys relationships.

We have little hope of being any different, apart from experiencing firsthand the transforming power and love of God. People with the best intentions simply do not consistently practice the Golden Rule principle without having had this selfish nature changed by an encounter with Jesus Christ.

Looking Ahead

As we proceed in studying the fine art of getting along with others, we will expand on "Treat others as you want to be treated." The chapters to come will include more than sixty principles that build on this Golden Rule, and these will unlock the door to success in all your relationships.

Remember, there is no limit to the success you enjoy when you follow this guideline Jesus gave us.

·························· **IN A CAPSULE** ··························

• **Principle 1** •

"Treat others as you want to be treated."

 PART I

Getting Along Means Reaching Out to Others

Opening Up

Five steps to set you free to
relate well to others

Someone has said, "If you don't love yourself, your neighbor is in big trouble." Before we can successfully reach out to others, we have to have a clear view of ourselves.

I once counseled with a woman called Karen Mae, who had no love for herself. Dan, who was married to her for seven years, admits he does not know who she is and said, "When I was married to Karen Mae, I repeatedly told her how much I loved her, but she never believed it."

Although Karen Mae might appear vivacious and outgoing at a party, after the band goes home, she quickly turns into the silent victim of her own low self-esteem. *Who is Karen Mae?* She wonders.

Karen Mae has had many acquaintances across the years, but no lasting one-on-one relationships. Playing hide-and-seek with her true feelings, she never allows another to get close to her.

This poor, lonely woman sought to become somebody by having an affair. But her attempt to build self-esteem ended up making her feel crummier than ever about herself. Devastated, she destroyed her marriage, blaming everything on her husband, Dan, and divorcing him.

She stubbornly refuses to admit that anything is wrong with her, yet Karen still thinks of herself as worthless. Wrapped up in her own miserable self, she does not relate well to others. Her feelings of inadequacy cause her to be harsh and critical of people; her fear of not being accepted and wanted rules her relationships. Divorcing Dan solved nothing: she still faces her low opinion of herself.

Karen Mae is only one of many closed persons. A *closed person* may be defined as one who feels so crummy about himself that he cannot relate well to other people. On the other hand, an *open person* has enough self-acceptance and feeling of worth to be free to reach out and relate well to other people.

Before we can practice the Golden Rule principle, "Treat others as you want to be treated," we must feel good about ourselves. How can we treat others as we want to be treated until first we decide and learn to treat ourselves well?

J. Martin Kohe, in his fabulous book *Your Greatest Power*, tells about an explorer who went to the wilds of Africa. He took a number of trinkets along for the natives. Among them were two full-length mirrors. He placed these mirrors against two trees and sat down to talk to some of his men about the exploration.

While talking, the explorer noticed that a native approached the mirror with a spear in his hand. As he looked into the mirror, he saw his reflection. He began to jab his "opponent" in the mirror, as though it were a real man, going through all the motions of killing him. Of course he broke the mirror into bits.

Seeing this, the explorer walked over to the man and asked why he had smashed the mirror. The native replied, "He go kill me. I kill him first."

All the trouble was with the native himself. It was caused by his faulty thinking. When it comes to getting along, most of our problems are caused because we are our own worst enemies. If we are to successfully master the art of getting along, we must first overcome our low self-esteem.

How do you become a more open person? How do you get comfortable with who you are so that you can be comfortable in reaching out and relating well to other people?

A few summers ago on a warm evening, my best friend and wife, Margi, and I spent some time alone together in Portland's west hills, where the rose garden is located. What a breathtaking spot of beauty! From this vantage point you can look out over the beautiful city of Portland, with all of its spectacular modern skyscrapers. Beyond, on the horizon, towering above it all, is the wonder of the Northwest, majestic Mount Hood. People come from all over the world, to this spot surrounded by giant firs, to walk through the Portland Rose Gardens.

As Margi and I walked hand in hand through the gardens, with all the infinite varieties of roses, we were captured by the beauty of it all—row after row of budding flowers of every color in the rainbow.

As we walked I noticed that some were in full bloom, while others remained in tight buds. A rose only becomes beautiful and blesses others when it opens up and blooms. Its greatest tragedy is to stay in a tight-closed bud, never fulfilling its potential.

This made me think about all the people in the world who are like the rosebud, bound up, their beauty hidden. Only as a flower receives the sunlight can it gain strength to open up and bloom.

If you have been a closed person, it's my prayer that as you study this chapter, the warm rays of God's love will penetrate to your innermost being. May you feel so accepted in the security of His unconditional love that you will open up, set free to bloom in the beauty of warm relationships with other people.

In my own journey to becoming a more open person I have discovered five basic, universal principles that have helped me to enjoy relating to others.

Five Steps to Set You Free to Relate Well to Others

Step 1: Be Willing to Change. If you could be guaranteed more enjoyable and lasting relationships with other people by changing some things, would you do so? We all have a natural impulse to resist change, and when it involves ourselves, we resist even more vehemently. Think through that self-defense and break out of it! By becoming willing to open yourself up to change, you have everything to gain, when it comes to winning friends and influencing people, and nothing to lose. The better you are willing to become, the more people are going to like you.

No less of a figure in history than Benjamin Franklin learned and benefited from being willing to change. When he was ambassador to France, he was the most sought-after man in Paris. But was Franklin always so popular? On the contrary. In his autobiography he describes himself as a blundering young man—uncouth and unattractive.

In Philadelphia one day an old Quaker friend took the young man aside and lashed him with these words: "Ben, you are impossible. Your opinions have a slap in them for everyone who differs with you. They have become so expensive nobody cares for them. Your friends find they enjoy themselves better when you're not around."

To Franklin's benefit he accepted this smarting rebuke. He understood that he needed to change, and change he did. Principle one can also work for your lasting benefit:

• Principle 1 •
You can change!

According to psychiatrist Rollo May, we choose not to change until we hurt intensely enough.

A human being will not change his personality pattern, when all is said and done, until he is forced to do so by his own suffering. . . . In fact, many neurotic individuals prefer to endure the misery of their present situation rather than to risk the uncertainty that would come with change.

A while back, Chuck Swindoll, on his national radio program, began his daily talk by reading these words from a book:

Having lost all sense of time, I wandered aimlessly along an unknown beach in the State of Washington. I was sobbing uncontrollably every step of the way. As the sun was going down and darkness was closing in, I dropped down on the beach completely exhausted. For me the sun had stopped shining; there was only darkness.

"Where the hell are you, God?" I shouted. Just a few brief months before, I would not have believed any true minister of God would think such words, let alone shout them angrily again and again at the top of his voice.

Anyone who has been broken apart emotionally by some shattering experience, be it the death of a loved one, financial disaster, a runaway son or daughter, a physical setback, or the most shattering of all emotional crises—divorce—knows what I mean when I say there was a pain inside me that cut like a knife.

At 31, my life was filled with success and all the things that I wanted most out of life. After two very successful pastorates, I was now pastor of one of the larger churches in our denomination in the State of Oregon. After I had been there only 13 months, the church doubled in all areas, and was starting to fulfill some of the dreams that I had. I had a wife whom I loved and had been married to since our freshman days in college. If anyone had asked me just a few months earlier, I would have told them that we had a happy marriage. I had an eight-year-old son, who was my pride and joy and everything I could want in a boy, and a little girl five years of age, who had a way of wrapping her fingers around my heart.

Then came that fateful day in October when my wife told me that she did not love me, that she never had, and that she was going to take the children and leave me forever, moving 2,500 miles away to her hometown in Ohio. She announced to me that I was the loser and that I would lose everything. I would lose the privilege of pastoring a church I loved, I would lose the wife whom I cherished and loved, and I would lose my two beautiful children. There would be nothing left for me.

In the following weeks and days I struggle desperately to try to save the sinking ship, all to no avail. Before ending up on that beach, at the bottom emotionally, I had gone four days without food, fasting and praying, calling on God to, by some miracle, save our marriage. Now, as I lay on the beach, I knew the marriage was over. My life as a minister would soon be wrecked. My children would be taken many miles away from me. Never before had we had a divorce in my immediate family and I didn't see how any of the family could ever accept me again.

My father, whom I loved and for whom I had great respect, had not only been a minister for as long as I could remember, but had for the past 30 years been the head administrator of our denomination in the State of Ohio. My dad's brother had also been a prominent minister. Both my grandfathers had helped to pioneer, and had literally sacrificed everything they had to help establish, the denomination that our family now enjoyed so very much. I grew up knowing how the church thought almost as well as I knew my own thoughts. Instinctively, I knew that there was no way that the people from this conservative, evangelical background would ever be able to understand my divorce. I would forever be, in their eyes, a "second-class citizen."

Chuck Swindoll concluded by saying, "Here is a man who knows pain and the depth of loneliness." It was from my book *Rebuild Your Life* that he read.

Would you agree that I needed a change? Up until this time I had been like the unopened rosebud. I had been a closed person, but now with a broken marriage relationship, the pain was unbearable. So I opened up to God's Spirit and said yes to the work He wanted to do in my personality.

I became intensely aware that I needed to change, that here was an opportunity for some tremendous growth in me as a person. My pain forced me to search out some very basic truths of Scripture. I rediscovered that as God's child I had worth and value. In spite of my humanness, God gave me the insight to start accepting myself unconditionally.

Experiencing this new acceptance, I was able to open up to faults and began to work on them, one by one. Then I discovered the freedom not only to admit when I was wrong but to share some of my own humanity with other people. As I became transparent with other people, I found myself growing in some pretty fantastic, wonderful new relationships.

Today, years later, I enjoy a very close relationship with my best friend and wife, Margi. I enjoy another eight or ten really close friendships. Besides this, I have the joy of warm relationships with many people. Now, if God can make all this change in me, what do you think He can do for you, if you will be willing to open up to change?

Because you have failed in a relationship, or several relationships, does not mean you are a hopeless failure. But it does mean that you need to open up to change and grow so that you can start succeeding in relationships. If you are now willing to change, you have taken the first step to set you free to relate well to others.

Step 2: Think of Yourself the Way God Thinks of You. How do you honestly think of yourself? We call this your self-image, and it determines how you act and relate to other people. Long ago the Bible said, "What a man thinks is really what he is" (Prov. 23:7 AP). A man rejects himself, so he rejects others. If a person feels unsure of himself, he's unsure of others. If one does not accept himself, he rarely accepts anyone else. The bottom line is this: If you cannot love yourself, you cannot freely reach out and love others. A good healthy dose of self-love can help loose every bound-up person.

Dr. William Glasser, author and founder of Reality Therapy, says, "All psychological problems, from the slightest neurosis to the deepest psychosis, are merely symptoms of the frustration of the fundamental need for a sense of personal worth. Self-esteem is the basic element in the health of any human personality."

Jesus, the greatest teacher of all time, realized this full well. Asked what was the most important of all commandments, Jesus replied, "Love the Lord your God with all your heart, soul, mind and strength." "Second," said Jesus, "love your neighbor as you love yourself" (see Mark 12:28–31). Our love for ourselves and for our neighbors should be second only to our love for God. That shows the importance of right thinking and good feelings about ourselves.

Our faulty thinking keeps us from fulfilling this goal. I want to challenge you to think correctly about yourself. A person does not do that until he begins to see himself from God's viewpoint. Our heavenly Father knows us without any exception and without any lies. He looks at us and sees us exactly as we are. Now how does God think about you as a person?

God Thinks You Have Tremendous Worth

Perhaps you feel unworthy of love. If so, change your thought patterns! When you think this way, you degrade yourself and ignore God's gift of worth, given to you when you were born.

But if God sees you as worthy, why don't you automatically see yourself that way? For many people, those negative emotions result from sin or sin's effects on their lives. Nothing in this world makes a person feel crummy about himself the way sin does.

The other day I thought about how much my house is worth. I may set a price on my house, but that doesn't really tell how much it's worth. The county tax appraiser has set a value on my house. That still really doesn't tell you how much it's worth. My house or any other property is worth only as much as someone is willing to pay for it. What a person actually gives for property determines its value.

Look what a price God paid for us. "For God so loved the world, that he gave his only begotten Son, that whosoever believeth in him should not perish, but have everlasting life" (John 3:16). After reading this verse, you should never doubt the value and worth God assigns you. God gave *everything* when He gave His only Son, Jesus, that you might be with Him for eternity.

Out of God's love, proven toward me, comes a tremendous sense of worth. Because God loves me, I am loved and I have value. How liberating it is to know that I am worth loving.

The time has come for you to take the second step in getting free to relate well to others. Practice the Bible principle that comes out of everything God did for us when Jesus died on the cross:

• Principle 2 •

Love yourself as God loves you.

Step 3: Treat Yourself as a Best Friend. How can you be your own best friend? By looking out for Number One, because you really can't count on anyone else? No! This secular approach, propagated by various unbelievers, is pure selfishness! Instead of resulting in the warm, lasting relationships that we desire, it disintegrates them.

Then how *do* you act as your own best friend? By treating yourself as you would your best friend. The secret of getting along is to practice Jesus' Golden Rule: "Treat others as you want to be treated." This principle assumes that you already treat yourself in a good manner. It's basic: You've got to begin by treating yourself right before you can treat others right.

Thinking this through, what is the best thing you can do for *other* people? What can you do to help them feel comfortable with you? How can you make them feel really important? What will let them know that they are okay in spite of their faults? It is something that we all long for from other people: We want to be accepted without conditions. The best thing you can do for *yourself*, which will set you free to relate, is to practice this principle:

• **Principle 3** •

Accept yourself unconditionally.

Carol Chalmers wanted to know: "How can I accept myself unconditionally with all that's wrong with me?"

In response to this honest confession and inquiry, I answered, "Carol, you are not supposed to accept your sins, nor are you to accept your faults, but you're supposed to accept yourself as being an okay, worthwhile, beautiful person. Yes, unacceptable things remain in your life, but you, yourself, are an acceptable person."

Carol said, "That all sounds good, but on what biblical basis can I do this?"

I picked up *The Living Bible* and from it shared these words: "When we were utterly helpless with no way of escape, Christ came at just the right time and died for us sinners who had no use for him. Even if we were good, we really wouldn't expect anyone to die for us, though, of course, that might be barely possible. But God showed his great love for us by sending Christ to die for us while we were still sinners" (Rom. 5:6–8).

Then I shared this favorite story with my seeking friend.

"Do you like dollies?" the little girl asked her house-guest.

"Yes, very much," the man responded.

"Then I'll show you mine," was the reply. Thereupon she presented one by one a whole family of dolls.

"And now tell me," the visitor asked, "which is your favorite doll?"

The child hesitated for a moment and said, "You're quite sure you like dollies, and will you please promise not to smile if I show you my favorite?"

The man solemnly promised, and the girl hurried from the room. In a moment she returned with a tattered and dilapidated old doll. Its hair had come off; its nose was broken; its cheeks were scratched; an arm and a leg were missing. "Well, well," said the visitor, "and why do you like this one best?"

"I love her most," said the little girl, "because if I didn't love her, no one else would."

I continued, "You see, Carol, this illustrates exactly how God loves each of us, and because of His unconditional love, we are also accepted unconditionally. His acceptance is not something we deserve, something we improve ourselves into, but it is a gift from God that we are to accept. And accepting the gift means accepting yourself as you are right now."

Accepting yourself unconditionally means accepting your own humanity. No one is perfect, and none of us have arrived in the state of sinlessness. Name the great Christian leaders today—all have their weaknesses, their humanity. If you don't believe it, just ask their mates or people who work with them every day.

Being kind to yourself and accepting your own humanity frees you to feel okay about yourself while you continue to grow into everything the name *Christian* means. This brings a new freedom to be happy with yourself. The Bible promises, "There is therefore now no condemnation to them which are in Christ Jesus" (Rom. 8:1). In other words, you are forgiven and set free from the bondage of guilt, while still working on your shortcomings. What good news!

Unconditional acceptance can set you free from playing the defeating comparison game. I remember the joy of success I felt when I wrote my first book and it was published. Then I made the mistake of beginning to compare myself with other, seasoned, better-known authors. Before I knew it, my joy had evaporated, and I felt crummy about myself and my abilities as a writer. You see, I was doing something God never intended for me to do. As a writer, I am not to be like anyone else. I am to be myself.

Accepting yourself unconditionally means that you become free to be you. We read, "Be honest in your estimate of yourselves, measuring your value with how much faith God has given to you" (Rom. 12:3 TLB). Accept your abilities and your liabilities. Get comfortable with yourself and then, with God's help, work on improving that self: *you*!

Step 4: Find Freedom by Opening Up to Your Faults. Naomi's husband bears witness that her critical spirit and cutting tongue make life almost unbearable for him. Her children will do almost anything to keep from being at home when she's there, because of the coarse way she treats them. Naomi has lost one job after another because of her inability to get along with people at work. Yet when you talk to her, as I have, she harangues and blames everyone but herself for all the trouble in her relationships. I've never known her to admit to one fault or mistake. She takes no responsibility at all for the broken relationships that keep occurring in her life. The Bible says, "A man who refuses to admit his mistakes can never be successful. But if he confesses and forsakes them, he gets another chance" (Prov. 28:13 TLB).

Everyone makes mistakes. Some will not admit it, however, and go on repeating the same mistakes. Thank God, we *can* admit when we are wrong and work hard at correcting our faults. Saint Augustine said, "The confession of evil works is the first beginning of good works."

Don't fool yourself. Instead practice this principle:

• **Principle 4** •

When you're wrong, admit it.

In Genesis, we see the first man, Adam, and the first woman, Eve, enjoying the freedom of an open, transparent relationship with each other and with God. There existed no deceit, no deception, and no guilt. Everything was open and aboveboard. They had no need to be defensive. Free from fear, they related with each other out of perfect love.

Then it happened: Adam and Eve chose to rebel against God and committed the first sin. Immediately the way they related changed for the worse.

The first hide-and-seek game started. We read:

> They hid themselves among the trees. The Lord God called to Adam. "Why are you hiding?"
>
> And Adam replied, "I heard you coming and didn't want you to see me naked. So I hid."
>
> "Who told you you were naked?" the Lord God asked. "Have you eaten fruit from the tree I warned you about?"
>
> Genesis 3:8–11 TLB

Why did Adam and Eve hide? Because they didn't want God to see their sin. They felt crummy about themselves. That's what sin does to people. So they "hid themselves among the trees."

In trying to hide our sins, we play many cover-up games. One of the most destructive in human relationships is the blame game. Blaming others for everything without accepting any responsibility for our wrongs ruins relationships. It puts everybody involved on the alert, like an atomic, battle-ready submarine poised to attack and destroy.

The destructive blame game is as old as Adam and Eve. While they were hiding behind the tree, trying to cover up their sin, God called them to account for what they'd done. Adam said, "It wasn't my fault; it was the woman!" And what did Eve say? "It wasn't my fault; the snake made me eat the fruit" (see Gen. 3:12, 13).

Recently, while rereading Dale Carnegie's book *How to Win Friends and Influence People*, I came across several illustrations of noted criminals of the thirties, such as Dutch Schultz, the New York mobster, Al Capone, the notorious Chicago killer, and "Two-gun" Crowley, who killed a Long Island policeman in cold blood. These three shared one especially interesting factor. They all claimed that they hadn't done anything wrong and blamed everyone else. Listen to what Al Capone said: "I have spent the best years of my life in giving people the lighter pleasure, helping them have a good time, and all I get is abuse, the existence of a hunted man." Al Capone was one of the most violent, destructive gangsters who has ever lived.

As a counselor, I have observed an amazing phenomenon. Nine times out of ten a person who has committed adultery against a marriage partner tries to justify the behavior by blaming the mate: "She was cold and unresponsive to me," or "He didn't give me the attention I needed." You see, the blame game is a way of saying, "I'm not responsible. I'm just the innocent victim."

James McCord, president of Princeton Theological Seminary, said, "To sin is man's condition. To pretend he is not a sinner, that is man's sin."

To open up about your sin and failure is one of the most healthy, freeing things you can do. Bruce Larson, in his book *There's a Lot More to Health Than Not Being Sick*, points out that our health and well-being are conditional upon being able to admit out loud: "I was wrong, please forgive me." Those who learn to confess and receive forgiveness have healthier bodies.

Confession also frees us from guilt. And being free from guilt releases us to relate openly with one another; we need not worry about being found out.

People who won't admit they're wrong are the hardest ones to live with. And the one person you have to live with is yourself. Before you can reach out and really enjoy others, you have to feel free within your own spirit. So do yourself a big favor: When you're wrong, admit it.

Step 5: Care Enough for Yourself to Share Yourself. John Powell, in his classic book entitled *Why Am I Afraid to Tell You Who I Am?* answers his own question, "I'm afraid to tell you who I am, because if I tell you who I am, you will not like who I am, and it's all that I have." We all have this fear that if people really know us they won't like us. In reality the exact opposite is the truth. The more a person shares his true self openly with us, the more we are drawn to him. As you have no doubt experienced, we more easily identify with a person who shares something of his or her humanity than we relate to a braggart. We cannot afford to surrender the leadership of our lives to our fears of not being accepted. Jesus came teaching us that there was a better way to live and relate. We are not to relate out of fear, but out of love. "For God hath not given us the spirit of fear; but of power, and of love, and of a sound mind" (2 Tim. 1:7).

Jesus taught us by example to open up and disclose ourselves to one another. He said, "I no longer call you slaves, for a master doesn't confide in his slaves; now you are my friends, proved by the fact that I have told you everything the Father told me" (John 15:15 TLB). Christ is not only our example, but our inward strength to reach out and share ourselves with others. Because He loves me and accepts me, I can love and accept myself and feel good enough about myself to share with others. To get beyond yourself and reach out and begin to develop close relationships, practice this principle:

• **Principle 5** •

Open up yourself to others, and
they will be drawn to you.

A new freedom in relating is experienced by individuals who dare to start sharing themselves openly and transparently with others. I remember Dr. Henry Jones and his wife and the very close relationship they enjoyed. But it wasn't always that way. During the first ten years of their marriage, each of them kept everything inside. They only talked about surface things and the bare essentials of life. They never dreamed of sharing their deep inner feelings with each other. What a lonely way to live together!

Then my friend Dr. Jones got involved in a Christian fellowship group. Over a period of months he learned to open himself up and allow the other men in the group to get to know him. Out of this, two things happened. First, he experienced release from the bondage he had felt inside. Second, for the first time in his life he was drawn into deep friendship with other men.

Based on what happened in the small group, Dr. Jones decided he wanted the same kind of thing in his marriage. He started opening up and sharing his feelings with his wife. At first, she could not give him any response. But he kept opening himself up to her anyway. After six months, she began to venture into this new area and share her feelings with her husband. Across the years this deep revealing between the Joneses developed, until now anyone who is around them very long can see that they enjoy a close communion. Aren't close relationships what we all want?

If this is not yet happening in your relationships, it can. You, too, can begin to open up and share yourself with others. And as you do, you are going to experience a freedom to be yourself, while reaching out to relate to others in a new, fulfilling way.[1]

Now that you know the five steps to set you free to relate well—and the principles on which they are based—you are ready to move on in our journey of reaching out to others.

·············· **IN A CAPSULE** ··············

• Principle 1 •

You can change!

• Principle 2 •

Love yourself as God loves you.

• Principle 3 •

Accept yourself unconditionally.

• Principle 4 •

When you're wrong, admit it.

• Principle 5 •

*Open up yourself to others, and
they will be drawn to you.*

1. For further teaching and discussion on the concept of self-love, see these four books: Dale Galloway, *Rebuild Your Life* (Wheaton, Ill.: Tyndale, 1975); Dale Galloway, *You Can Win with Love* (Eugene, Ore.: Harvest House, 1976); Dale Galloway, *How to Feel like a Somebody* (Eugene, Ore.: Harvest House, 1978); Stanley C. Baldwin, *A True View of You* (Ventura, Calif.: Regal, 1982).

Give People What They Need

*The five principles you need to know
to get along with others*

Our New Hope Community Church was full to overflowing. People packed the pews like sardines in a can, and several hundred others had to find seats in the overflow area. During twenty-three years of ministry, I had never witnessed a larger funeral.

This was the memorial service for my good friend Harry Vawter. Sitting on the platform listening to Harry's minister son, Dr. John Vawter, pay tribute to his father's life, I couldn't help but ask, *Why are more than one thousand people here at this funeral service?*

Harry Vawter was not a well-known public figure or even an extrovert. Basically a rather shy man, over lunch one day Harry confided that he had fought feelings of inferiority all his life. But he did not allow this to stop him from going beyond and reaching out to others.

What caused so many people to attend the funeral? And why were so many deep expressions of love and friendship spoken to the family members? How could this one man influence all these lives in such a warm, positive way?

Harry had discovered the secret of how to get along with people. He practiced the Golden Rule principle: "Treat others as you want to be treated." In doing this he made people feel good about themselves. The more you create, enhance, and reinforce self-esteem in other people, the better they are going to like you. My friend Harry understood this and practiced it in his daily relationships with others.

As you learn to understand other people so that you can build them up as persons, you're going to create a happier living environment for everyone. People are so much easier to live with, work with, and get along with when they have good feelings about themselves. So as you build the self-esteem level of the

Making other people feel good about themselves is like putting money in the bank. It pays rich dividends.

people you relate to, you're actually making it easier for yourself to get along with them. You're on the beam when you build someone's self-esteem.

I teach our staff pastors and lay pastors that when people act weird and seem difficult to get along with, you've got to take the time to find out where they're coming from and what is going on in their lives. You can't treat other people the way they want to be treated until you know what they need.

In working with church boards, I have learned the valuable lesson that it pays to take the time before conducting business to find out where people are and what's going on in their lives. On our church board we have found that a period of time spent in sharing with one another and praying for one another creates a loving, understanding atmosphere in which to conduct the business of the church. As a young pastor many years ago, I learned the hard way that when people have unsolved problems or conflict or misunderstandings in their personal life, it affects their decision-making processes as members of a board.

To get along well with people, you will need to become an alert student, studying their feelings and needs. Realize that everyone has the same basic needs that you have. Here are some of them:

1. Love given and received
2. Food, shelter, and preservation of life
3. A feeling of importance

4. A sense of being needed and useful
5. Money and the things money will buy
6. Life after death
7. Health and happiness
8. The well-being of children and family members
9. A craving for fellowship and oneness with God

But what is the deepest need of every human being? Sigmund Freud, the father of psychology, taught that everything you and I do springs from two natures: the sex urge and the desire to be great. John Dewey, the leader in the philosophy of American education, said, "The deepest urge in human nature is the desire to be important." Dr. Robert Schuller, speaker on a successful national Christian television program, "Hour of Power," says, "The will to self-love is the deepest of all desires." When you sum up, what these leaders in psychology, philosophy of education, and religion are saying is that the greatest need we have as human beings is expressed in this principle:

• Principle 1 •

Everyone needs to feel like a somebody!

After a busy Christmas season and a hectic post-season schedule, my wife, Margi, gave me a needed birthday present—two days away at a mountain retreat cabin. On my birthday, we who are best friends shared the joy of relaxing, relating, and resting. It was like finding an oasis after many days of traveling in a hot desert sun.

While away on our retreat, we left our two children, Scott and Ann, in the care of Grandpa and Grandma Watson. Upon our return Saturday afternoon, we heard the good news that the children had enjoyed a wonderful time, as did Grandpa and Grandma.

Grandpa Watson told of taking eight-year-old Ann to the nearby shopping center to purchase some bedroom slippers. After having gotten exactly what she wanted, Ann looked up at her Grandpa Watson, who towers six feet five inches, and said with big eyes and true sincerity of heart, "You're the best grandpa in the whole world." As if that wasn't enough, she added, "I really love you, and don't know what I'd do without my special grandpa."

As Grandpa related the happy experience to us, it was easy to tell that Ann was not the only one who had received a special gift. Here's an eight-year-old little girl who is already enriching her relationships by practicing this number-one principle, "Everyone needs to feel like a somebody."

Whenever You Help a Person Feel Like a Somebody, He Will Like You for It!

I believe that even the most struggling person's life could be changed for the better if someone would reach out and make him feel like a somebody. One of the ways that you and I can serve our heavenly Father is to help His other children discover their true worth and value.

Some years ago a boy of ten worked in a factory in Naples. He had a burning desire to be a great singer, but his first teacher wiped him out by saying, "You can't sing." Then to add insult to injury, the teacher said, "You have no voice at all. It sounds like the wind in the shutters."

Fortunately, this boy's mother, who was but a poor peasant, had the good sense to believe in her son and his capabilities to fulfill the burning desire of his heart. She put her arms around him, nursed his wounds, and encouraged him not to give up. She praised him by telling him that she loved to hear him sing and that as he worked hard at it he would improve and become a great singer. This mother backed up her belief in her son by going barefoot herself in order to save money to pay for his music lessons.

That mother's belief in her son and her praise gave the boy the courage to pursue his dream. His name? Enrico Caruso, one of the greatest operatic tenors of all time.

Build another person up by believing in him, and you will become a partner in his achievements. Almost everyone responds warmly to the person who reaches out to give him or her a needed boost. Encourage others to be everything that they can be. They will love you for it, and your relationships will be enriched with growing friendship.

People Are Different

On a hot summer day an elegant restaurant in Europe was having some difficulty with flies. Dining there were an Englishman, a Scotchman, and an Irishman, and each had a fly land right in the middle of his soup.

The English have a lot of class. When the fly landed in the Englishman's soup, he glanced around to make sure no one was looking, so he wouldn't embarrass anyone. Then he gracefully took his silver spoon and gently retrieved the fly from his soup, placed it in the ashtray, then covered the dripping corpse with his linen napkin. He gave it a royal burial!

When the fly landed in the Irishman's soup, being a man of strong feelings, he saw that it was time for action. He drew a deep breath and blew with all his might, blowing the fly right out of the soup and also blowing half the soup out of his bowl. The Irish are expressive.

As the story goes, the fly landed in the Scotchman's soup, and for a long time he watched it swimming around in his bowl. Finally he motioned the waiter to come over and said, "What's this fly doing in my soup?"

The waiter looked and said, "I think it's the back-stroke, sir."

Pretty soon, the fly stopped swimming. At that point, the Scotchman reached down and grabbed it by the wings, lifted it about two inches above the bowl, shook it as hard as he could, and said, "Okay, spit it out! Spit it out!"

As this anecdote illustrates: People are different! They vary in their heritage, in their upbringing, in their temperaments, in their personalities, and in the way they look and think. A large family has no one child just like another. In reaching out to understand and get along with other people, accept principle number two:

• Principle 2 •

No two people are alike.

A rather large percentage of the misunderstandings that occur between people directly result from a lack of understanding concerning basic differences. Whenever we do not recognize and respect the other person's right to be different, we have already created the climate for not getting along.

Tim LaHaye, a well-known Christian writer, has been noted for his teaching on temperaments. In *Spirit-Controlled Temperament* he describes four major ones:

1. Sanguines are extroverts—optimistic and always talking. They are outgoing, chatty, expressive, and not worried about details. A person with this temperament can be forgetful.

2. Cholerics—also extroverts and optimists, these people's goal in life is to "get it done." Decisive, born leaders, they want the job done now, and the quicker the better. Words like *driver*, *dominating*, *impatient* characterize cholerics, who have a tendency to become workaholics. At the same time, cholerics achieve much.

3. Melancholies, deep and thoughtful people, often show talent, creativity, and giftedness in art and music. They are perfectionists and very sensitive in their feelings. A melancholy can drive other people a little bit batty with his meticulous standards for housekeeping. Also melancholies are prone to moodiness and can quickly fall into depression.

4. Phlegmatics, introverts and pessimists by nature, may be characterized by words such as *calm*, *easygoing*, and *relaxed*. They never get in a hurry about anything, but just keep plodding along.

These temperament descriptions are not precise and will vary with the individual. Most of us will uniquely blend several of these types. However, usually each of us inclines toward one.

A few months ago, in one of our church pastoral staff meetings, I led a study of different temperaments.

It was fascinating to discover that every one of the seven on the pastoral team had a distinct and different mixture of temperaments. Just talking about our varied temperaments gave us additional understanding for working together as a team.

I confess that the only difficulty that I have ever had in years of working as senior pastor occurred when I started expecting a fellow pastor to be like me. As long as I allow each pastor to be himself, while we relate and work together on the same goals, we get along beautifully. That's my confession. How much room do you give people you work with to be different in temperament from you?

Repeatedly in my pastoral counseling I have seen serious rifts come between a husband and a wife simply because they did not know that males and females have very different reproductive drives. Not understanding this, they got into a negative cycle. Neither one was meeting the other person's needs, and consequently neither one was having his or her needs met.

The wife says, "He doesn't love me, he doesn't understand me, he doesn't even begin to meet my emotional needs. All he ever wants is my body. He's an animal."

The husband's side of the story? He says, "Look, I work my fool head off supporting that woman and our kids. What more does she want from me?" The upset husband continues, "She never has time for me. Her mind is always occupied with the children or something else. It's just my luck to marry a frigid woman. It's a terrible thing to feel rejected."

The wife responds, "I cook for him, I iron his clothes, make his bed, do his laundry, take care of his kids, work at a job to help support this family. What more does he want?"

I can't tell you how many times I've seen this negative cycle repeated in the lives of good people who, at one time, really loved each other. Who's right and who's wrong? They're both right, and they're both wrong. But neither one understands that males and females are different from each other. Because of the variation in psychological and physical drives, men and women come from very different viewpoints.

The female, by her very makeup, naturally focuses on her nesting and maternal activities. She has an enormous need to feel secure. She looks to her husband to meet her emotional needs by caring enough to listen to her and by accepting her as being okay. When the wife's emotional needs are met, and only then, does she become responsive sexually.

On the other hand, the male's reproductive drive centers on sex. A wife can do everything else for him, but unless she's responsive to his sexual advances, he's going to feel rejected, wounded in his ego, and unloved. As you might know from firsthand experience, all kinds of misunderstandings arise because the male approaches the female from the male viewpoint and because the female approaches the male from the female viewpoint.

What is the solution? It is to see that we are different and to put ourselves in the other person's shoes. This brings me to principle number three.

• Principle 3 •
Understanding begins with seeing it from the other person's point of view.

In a tremendous bit of advice on the fine art of human relations, Henry Ford said, "If there is any one secret of success, it lies in the ability to get the other person's point of view and see things from that person's angle as well as from your own."

Reaching Out Means Putting Yourself in the Other Person's Shoes

Two close friends who had a financial dispute asked me to meet with them and help settle their differences. I went against my better judgment and got smack in the middle of their disagreement. The first time I met with them, they both became so emotional in trying to push their own viewpoints that reason went out the window.

It did not take a genius to see that we were getting nowhere fast. Not wanting things to get out of hand any further, I called a truce. I asked each of them to go home and think about it for four days, and then we would meet again.

I was not looking forward with fond anticipation to the second meeting. In the minutes preceding my friends' arrival, I claimed the promise of Scripture that says, "If any of you lack wisdom, let him ask of God, that giveth to all men liberally" (James 1:5). I asked, wanting to know what God wanted me to do, and as I was communicating with Him an idea dropped into my mind.

As soon as my friends arrived, handing each of them a sheet of paper and a pen, I asked each to put himself in the other person's shoes and write down what he would settle for in that case. They looked at me for a moment as if to say, *You've got to be kidding*. But because they were both my friends and respected my judgment, they went ahead and did as I asked.

As they began to put themselves in each other's shoes, thinking from the other person's viewpoint, they wrote on the sheet of paper. I could feel the entire atmosphere change.

When they finished writing, I had them read their solutions aloud. Within two minutes they achieved compromise and a full settlement. Even better than that, there was a spirit of understanding and goodwill.

Reach Out to Other People by Trying to Understand Their Actions

This past Tuesday night something happened that scared me. I went to the church about 6:30 PM and approached the janitor's room to turn on the parking-lot lights for people coming to choir practice.

I put my key in the door, opened it, entered the small concrete room, not expecting anyone to be there, and walked right into a stranger. Adding to my alarm was the fact that he had earphones on and was plugged into our phone lines. I looked at him in not the most friendly way and demanded, "Who are you?"

"Oh," he said, "I'm from the phone company, and I'm working on your telephone lines." Still unconvinced, I asked him to show me some identification.

He reached into his pocket, pulled out his wallet, and showed me his identification card. Then I felt like a donkey. I confess that's not the first time I've jumped to a wrong conclusion.

Principle four is this:

• **Principle 4** •

Don't jump to conclusions.

I can't count the number of times I have violated principle four in my counseling sessions. After listening compassionately and intently to an unhappy marriage partner, I have made the fatal error of swallowing everything he or she has said hook, line, and sinker. Later I have discovered there was an opposite viewpoint, another side of the story. In Proverbs we read this rather humorous and yet true proverb, "Any story sounds true until someone tells the other side and sets the record straight" (Prov. 18:17 TLB).

On an airplane flight from Chicago to Los Angeles two boys aged about four and six were misbehaving. These two little monsters were yelling, screaming, hitting, biting, and generally disturbing the peace of anyone within four or five rows of them on the airplane. The man with them was beside himself, being unable to control the two children's behavior.

Finally one woman did what most of the other passengers watching wanted to do. She tapped the man on the shoulder and said, "Mister, why don't you control your kids?"

He replied, "Madam, I'm so sorry, but these children's father and mother were killed just two days ago in an automobile accident. I was their neighbor and am accompanying them to California to live with their grandparents." Immediately, everyone around who heard the explanation not only made allowances for the children's troublesome behavior, but even felt sympathy for them.

It can make a world of difference when you finally know what's going on in the other person's mind. Frequently I have found that the harsh word, the abrupt manner, the irritability goes deeper than what you can see on the surface at the moment. So often we just do not know what is going on in the other person's life. Inside he may be doing battle to cope with a tragedy, an illness, a heavy debt load, a child who's in trouble, or a whole group of things that together create an unbearable stress load. You cannot really understand another person until you get into his life, walk in his shoes, and feel what he feels.

Reach Out and Give the Other Person Acceptance

We all want and need to be accepted. This deep-seated desire makes us willing to do almost anything. I'll never forget some of the initiations that I went through as a kid. At about thirteen I went through one of the most excruciating experiences of my life. While my fellow caddies, whose approval I was trying to win, were using their belts on my backside, I pushed a golf ball up a steep hill of the eighteenth green, with my nose. I thought my nose was going to come off from rubbing in the dirt and on the ball. Yet I kept going up, up, up the hill, across the green, and finally, after what seemed like hours, into the hole. Then came the cheers. I was accepted. I belonged to the elite caddy group.

I do not believe we should make people go through such agony before accepting them. Do you? Jesus, our example, accepted people of all kinds just as they were. He was described as "a friend of tax collectors and sinners." He did not make them jump through hoops and then accept them. Jesus wants us to follow in His steps and do for each other what He did for us. The Bible teaches us to accept one another just as Christ accepts us.

Do you accept other people? What about those of a different religion, different race, or on a different social level? What about sinners? Our Lord accepted us, the Scriptures tell us, "while we were yet sinners" (Rom. 5:8).

One of the greatest things you can do for another person is to reach out and love that person as he is. Do that, and two very positive things happen. First, you create an atmosphere in which that person can improve and mature. Someone has said a warm human relationship is necessary to give a person the courage to face and understand his own mistakes. Knowing that someone loves him as he is enables him finally to face his own delusions and admit his need of change. By believing in another person, you help him become better.

This attitude produces a second result. Feeling your warmth, that person will be drawn to you. You will never want for friends if you observe this difficult yet essential principle number five:

* **Principle 5** *

Practice unconditional acceptance!

One of the best-known doctors in the world in the healing of the mind and soul is Dr. Paul Tournier. He lives in Geneva, Switzerland, and both ministerial students and young doctors come in a continual flow to Geneva to see this healer among men. They always want to know about his secret techniques. Says Dr. Tournier, "I have no methods. All I do is accept people."

We live in a fragmented, broken world. You can be God's healing agent if you refuse to surrender to your prejudices, to judging other people, and if you simply in the love of Christ reach out and accept people as they are.

Many of us never learn to distinguish between approval of behavior and acceptance of the person. When I talk about accepting a person unconditionally I am not meaning that you have to approve of the other person's attitudes or actions. What you do is to love the person as he is, despite his flaws.

For example, I believe my children are wonderful persons, but I certainly do not always approve of their attitudes or their behavior. Even when I must administer discipline to one of my children, I still let that child know that I value him or her, even with those weaknesses and feelings.

Stop Trying to Change the Other Person— Accept Him

Sometimes we can understand a principle by seeing its opposite. What is the opposite of practicing unconditional acceptance? It is trying to change the other person. In Keith Miller's classic book *Taste of New Wine*, he tells how he created tension in his marriage by trying to change his wife. Keith tells about his conversion and the two years when he was a Christian and his wife was not. He so desperately wanted to share his newfound joy and wonderful life in Christ with Mary Ellen. He tried every way he could think of to convince her that she should do the same thing he had done—commit her life to Jesus Christ. It seems perfectly logical that a husband who has been deeply committed to a living Christ should set about trying to get his wife converted. But the harder Keith Miller tried to convert his wife, the more cold and upset she became. Later, she told him that all she could hear him say was that they had been happily married for five years, and suddenly he didn't like her as she was, that he wasn't going to accept her fully unless she changed into some kind of religious fanatic.

Keith Miller said,

> Finally, I realized the unchristian pressure my trying to force Mary Ellen into my version of a Christian wife was having in her life. We were drifting apart. Although things looked happy on the surface, we both knew that our marriage was bruised and broken on the inside, where the world could not see. Finally, one night I said to her, "Honey, I can't deny the tremendous things which have happened to me these past two years, because of trying to give my future to the finding of God's will, but I have been wrong in trying to force all this on you. No one forced it on me. I'm sorry I tried (however unconsciously) to manipulate you by taking you to all these meetings, etc., to get you converted. I am really sorry." I went on to tell her, "When we got married I didn't sign up to change you, just to love you . . . and I do, just as you are."

I can change no other person by direct action.
I can change only myself.
When I change, others tend to change in response to me.

You talk about relieving the pressure valve. As a result of Keith's open confession and change in attitude, all the pressure that had been building up was gone, and there was relaxation and freedom once again in the Miller home. Within a few weeks Mary Ellen went out and made a beginning commitment of her future to Christ all by herself in a way that was right for her.

Whenever you try to force another person to change, you drive that person away from you. Save yourself a lot of frustration and bring a new sense of freedom and relaxation to all your relationships by practicing this universal law of mind and spirit.

Stop trying to change other people in your life. That is not what they need from you. They need acceptance. So why not give them what they need? Accept them as they are and encourage them to be themselves. They will love you for it. Remember, "love is not possessive" (see 1 Cor. 13:4). But love reaches out to give to others, and love is not only understanding, but magnanimous!

···················· **IN A CAPSULE** ····················

• Principle 1 •
Everyone needs to feel like a somebody!

• Principle 2 •
No two people are alike.

• Principle 3 •
*Understanding begins with seeing it from
the other person's point of view.*

• Principle 4 •
Don't jump to conclusions.

• Principle 5 •
Practice unconditional acceptance!

3

Make Relationships Last

*Four things you can do to make your
relationships continue*

Recently I talked to a middle-aged man who
divulged that he had been experiencing a
considerable amount of depression. When I
asked him about its cause, he poured out one sad
story after another about his closest friends getting divorces. This man felt brokenhearted over the
disintegration of relationships he and his wife had
valued for years and expected to continue. Suddenly
everything changed.

I heard the other day about two neighbors, closest
of friends for more than twenty years, who now won't
even speak to each other. Both have put their homes

up for sale so they won't have to live across the street from each other anymore.

These days one has to wonder if any relationships last. Their falling apart has become the most repeated and painful problem in our contemporary society.

The church is not some monastery, isolated from what's going on in the world. Christians are not exempt from the heartbreak of broken relationships. Few of us have not felt firsthand the excruciating pain resulting from a broken relationship.

Naturally we recognize that some relationships are not meant to continue for life. These exist for a short period of time simply because they fall in the people-user category and not the people-lover category. Sometimes we relate to people for what they are worth to us, for how they can meet our needs at some particular point. Sometimes this is perfectly appropriate.

For example, I am writing this section while flying to my home in Portland, Oregon, after having spoken at a large Bible conference in Massachusetts. There, for three busy, delightful days, a young man by the name of Jeff acted as my personal chauffeur. Jeff made sure I got to every speaking engagement and appointment on time. During our travels, we shared many conversations. A few hours ago he drove me to the airport. As enjoyable as our relationship was for a few days, I doubt we'll ever see each other again. The relationship was temporary by its very nature. But what about our more permanent relationships? How can we make them last?

Four Things You Can Do to Make Your Relationships Last

1. Practice Peacemaking. A little girl who had been spanked by her father climbed up into her mother's lap and said, "Mama, I wish you'd married Jesus; He loves little kids."

If you think and feel for yourself, your relationships are bound to be marked by conflict at times. Conflict naturally results when two people with their own minds and own feelings come together and relate.

In the introduction of David Augsburger's classic book *Caring Enough to Confront*, he says, "It is not the conflicts that need to concern us, but how conflicts are handled." Contrary to anything you've heard or naively believed, the Christian life is not immune to conflict. Every human being alive, Christian and non-Christian, experiences a variety of conflicts in every relationship of life.

The good news is that Jesus Christ, both by His teachings and life, has given to us the principles and the power to deal with conflict, not only creatively, but successfully.

Jesus said, "Blessed are the peacemakers: for they shall be called the children of God" (Matt. 5:9). Within these words Jesus gives to us principle number one for enjoying enduring relationships:

• **Principle 1** •

Be a peacemaker.

Not everyone in this world is a peacemaker. A friend I grew up with got me into a lot of trouble.

There was a boy in our class who was tough, and the kids in our school wanted to know who was toughest, me or the other guy. One of my supposedly good friends, unbeknownst to me, kept telling the other fellow that I said nasty things about him that I hadn't said. Then the instigator would come to me and tell me that the other tough guy was bragging how he was going to beat up on me. My friend, the instigator, kept right on agitating until the unsuspecting tough guys met in the middle of the playground to see who was the toughest and beat the daylights out of each other. I got drawn into conflict, and I got beat up on.

I suspect that there might be a little bit more of the troublemaker in some of us than we would like to admit.

But Jesus wants us to be peacemakers. This means that when conflict has occurred, causing misunderstanding and hard feelings, we don't sit around festering and pouting. As children of God, we take the initiative and do whatever we can to make peace with the person. The Bible is very clear that as Christians we are called to a ministry of reconciliation (see 2 Cor. 5:18). If that means humbling yourself, then that's what you do. In talking about being a peacemaker, I'm not talking about coddling people and giving in to them to keep peace at any price. Peacemaking must be balanced with caring enough to confront, which we'll talk about a little bit later on in this chapter.

On one of the news programs, it was reported that a couple had been remarried after fifty years, and one year into their new marriage they enjoyed each other so much. It was the happiest year of both of their lives.

The story went on to tell how fifty years before, when they were married, the man had been unfaithful. The injured wife, in her rage, divorced him. Now after all these years of being apart and finally coming back together she said, "It was my foolish pride that divorced him; it was my foolish pride that kept us apart all these years when we could have been enjoying each other's love."

A peacemaker goes the second mile. Jesus taught us that if a person asks you to go a mile, you should go two miles. To be a peacemaker, you've got to be willing to go that extra mile sometimes before the other person will budge an inch.

2. Work Out Your Unresolved Anger. A little boy and girl were talking. The little boy said, "What do you think of this devil business?"

The little girl answered, "I believe it's just like Santa Claus: it's our dad."

Though you might laugh at this, in real life it's not funny. The little girl really has some unresolved anger toward her father. And this type of anger does more to separate people from each other than any other cause.

Anger does not always result in one's blowing his top. Some of the most destructive kind of anger, never verbalized, ends in silent destruction.

Alan Loy McGinnis, in his popular book *The Friendship Factor*, says, "Passive hostility is a troublesome snake in the grass of friendship." This is why the Bible exhorts us, "Don't let the sun go down with you still angry—get over it quickly" (Eph. 4:26 TLB). From this we get a good-sense principle that makes not only for healthier bodies, minds, and souls, but enduring relationships:

• Principle 2 •

Work out your anger quickly.

Anger is like a hot potato: If you don't deal with it quickly, it burns you in your relationships. Experiencing anger is all a part of being human and living in relationships. Learn to handle it, and to do it quickly before it permanently damages the relationship!

In my book *Dare to Discipline Yourself*, in the chapter entitled "Understanding and Learning How to Handle Your Anger," I explain in detail nine principles to practice in getting a handle on your anger:

1. Confess it.
2. Trace the cause of your anger.
3. Accept personal responsibility for your anger.

4. Train yourself to hold your tongue until you cool down.

5. Work out your aggression in a healthy way.

6. Gain control by giving control to the Holy Spirit.

7. Don't nurse a grudge.

8. Be open and honest with the other person about what is stirring you up.

9. Set your spirit free by praying for the person who has injured you.

Here is how one grandmother dealt with her anger: A teenage grandchild visiting the home went out one night without telling anyone where she was going. When she came in, her grandmother's reaction stunned her. Angry, the grandmother said some venomous things that surprised even her. After all, the girl had only gone skating on their pond—by herself.

After the girl had gone to bed, the grandmother tried to see why she had reacted so unreasonably. She found that a series of small annoyances and fears in connection with her granddaughter had not been dealt with at once, but had been repressed. She had "forgotten" them. This last incident was one too many and brought all the others to the surface in an explosion all out of proportion to its cause.

The next day the grandmother told the girl what she had seen about herself—where she was wrong—and apologized for her outburst. She asked the girl to pray with her, which she did. This brought a new element into their relationship. The girl saw how thoughtless she had been and apologized.

This whole misunderstanding need never have happened if the grandmother had been open and honest, sharing her feelings naturally with the girl day by day. The incidents seemed so trivial in themselves that she had not wanted to mention them. They made her seem small. But because she bottled them up, they accumulated the force that ultimately caused that shameful explosion. Besides this, by not being honest with her granddaughter, she deprived her of the opportunity to learn to be more thoughtful and to change.

Handle your anger by preventing its buildup. Talk out things that irritate you and upset you before they get to the boiling point inside. This leads to the third thing that you can do to make your relationships last.

3. Care Enough to Confront. A man noted for his straightforward communication heard a noise in the night. When he got out of bed and investigated, he found a burglar in his house. He got his gun and stood quietly in the doorway and, pointing the gun at the burglar, softly said, "My friend, I wouldn't do you any harm, but you're standing where I'm about to shoot."

Your relationships will be only as good as your ability to communicate what you think and feel. Then you must be open to what the other person has to communicate.

Lasting relationships are based on an unbeatable combination of truth and love. Anything founded on less than openness and honesty is built on quicksand. Cicero said, "It appears then that genuine friendship cannot exist where one of the parties is unwilling to hear the truth and the other is equally indisposed to speak it."

The Bible says, "Let us speak the truth in love: so we shall fully grow up into Christ" (Eph. 4:15 NEB). The context of the verse talks about preaching the Word out of a heart of love, letting the chips fall where they may, so that fellow Christians might grow up in Christ. But we certainly do no harm to this interpretation by taking the principle a step further and applying it to confronting in love those to whom we relate.

There are no meaningful, enduring relationships without learning to practice this principle:

• Principle 3 •

Speak the truth in love.

According to our principle, the most healthy way to handle daily irritations is to get them out and talk them over in love.

Sometimes we hold another person accountable for our negative feelings, when he or she knows nothing about them. How unfair this is for everyone. For the good of all, when something bothers you, speak up and speak the truth in love. Handle your irritations daily, and you will avoid the big emotional blowups.

We are all prone to believe that communication of unfavorable emotional feelings makes waves. If I need to tell you that something you do bothers me, I may be tempted to think that it would be better not to mention it. Our relationship will be more peaceful, or I might think you wouldn't understand anyway. So I keep it inside myself. But each time you do something else, my stomach keeps score: two . . . three . . . four . . . five . . . six . . . seven . . . eight. . . . Then one day you do the same thing you've always done and my anger breaks loose. All the while you were annoying me, I kept it inside and somewhere, secretly, was learning to hate you.

When the explosion came, you didn't understand— and I may have surprised myself. It all started when I said, "I don't like what she's doing, but I'd better not say anything. The relationship will be more peaceful." What I did was not avoid trouble, but save up dynamite for the big explosion.

Only learning to speak the truth in love keeps conflict under control and from becoming open hostility. To speak the truth in love is to learn to report openly and honestly your own ideas and feelings. "I feel this way." "This is my viewpoint." "I don't know why this bothers me, but it does." In doing this you do not

> When you try to get even, you hurt yourself more than you hurt the other fellow.

blame the other person or make him out to be all wrong and yourself all right. You simply report on your own thoughts and feelings.

In practicing this principle, watch your timing. When you're ready may not be the best time for the other person. Sensitively consider the other person's problems. The day he's fired from his job, don't tell him something he does bothers you. Never use the truth like a sledgehammer to beat down another. Speak the truth through a heart of love that heals and builds up the other person and your relationship.

Before you speak the truth, love toward the other person must be in your heart. Get this love by spending time praying for him. As you pray check your own motives. Truth spoken out of love is never harsh, rude, or crude, but has as its goal better understanding.

This leads us to the fourth thing you can do to make your relationships last. Because of our humanness and mistakes, without this one no relationship could ever last.

4. Open Up the Fountain of Forgiveness. Fred is late again for dinner, and Norma is furious because her carefully prepared meal is ruined. Throughout the meal, they sit in silence. Fred feels guilty, but his pride doesn't let him say, "I'm sorry." Instead, he goes to the kitchen with Norma and helps her with the dishes and later puts up the hooks in the closet, which she's been asking him to tend to for weeks. All this substitutes for an honest apology.

Suppose that during the dinner, Fred had admitted his fault and said, "I'm sorry, dear. I could have phoned, and I should have when I knew I was going to be late. Will you please forgive me?" Then Norma would have responded with understanding and forgiveness. The tension would have been relieved with a great big kiss and love renewed once again.

Right now I am going to give what I believe to be one of the most important principles in human relationships. Mark it down. If you relate to another person long enough, sooner or later that person will hurt you in some way. That's a fact of life; that's the way it is! Practice this principle:

• **Principle 4** •

*There are no enduring relationships
without forgiveness.*

You need to know and understand the three things that happen when you use the healing power of forgiveness in your relationships—and when you refuse to use it:

An unforgiving spirit destroys, but forgiveness heals. Resentment and bitterness act on our spirits as poison does on our bodies. They infect our thoughts, damage our emotions, and make us sick. For this reason the Bible says, "Watch out that no bitterness takes root among you, for as it springs up it causes deep trouble" (Heb. 12:15 TLB).

There's absolutely no positive benefit to be gained by holding on to ill feelings toward another person.

They had been married for thirty-two years. It should have been the happiest time in their marriage. They had made it through the struggles of raising a large family, had all the children happily married, and were comfortable financially.

With a set jaw she poured out these words of hate. "I would rather rot in hell and see him dead than forgive him for what he's done with that other woman."

To my wounded friend, I said, "I understand your pain and hurt. I can even see why you would be bitter. But let me tell you, unless you forgive him, you're going to go on hurting in your spirit, and there is going to be destructiveness between you and your husband."

True to her word, she never forgave him. Oh, they went on living together, miserably. Every day they kept destroying each other. Finally he couldn't take it anymore, his heart gave out, and he died. Following his death, she carried not only resentment but an unbearable load of guilt mixed with hate. How different it could have been, if only she had practiced what Jesus taught us in the Lord's Prayer—to forgive others their trespasses (see Matt. 6:12).

Peter once asked Jesus, "How many times should we forgive?" Jesus went right to the heart of the matter when He told Peter to forgive seventy times seven (see Matt. 18:21, 22). He was not ministering to our souls, but saving our bodies from ulcers, colitis, high blood pressure, and all other kinds of diseases.

Practicing forgiveness releases it into our own lives. Jesus taught us that our forgiveness for people flows out of God's forgiveness toward us. We do this for others because God has done so much for us. Jesus also told us that God's pardon can depend on our being willing to overlook the faults of others. "For if ye forgive men their trespasses, your heavenly Father will also forgive you: But if ye forgive not men their trespasses, neither will your Father forgive your trespasses" (Matt. 6:14, 15).

If we stubbornly refuse to forgive another person, to heal another person in a broken relationship, then what we do is stop the flow of forgiveness and healing into our own lives. What you give is what you get:

> Try to show as much compassion as your Father does. Never criticize or condemn—or it will all come back on you. Go easy on others; then they will do the same for you. For if you give, you will get! Your gift will return to you in full and overflowing measure, pressed down, shaken together to make room for more, and running over. Whatever measure you use to give—large or small—will be used to measure what is given back to you.
>
> Luke 6:36–38 TLB

To paraphrase: If you forgive, you will be forgiven. If you are willing to heal all others, including your enemy, you will be healed. The condition of being healed of all emotional, physical, and spiritual illness is to do everything you can do to cast sin out of your life.

Jesus taught that you can't expect to have your prayers answered until you forgive your brother, until you do everything in your power, with God's help, to bring reconciliation to yourself and to the other person.

You're having trouble forgiving another person? I'll tell you what to do. Admit it to God. Open yourself up and ask God to give you the power and the love to break through the barrier and do it in Jesus' name. This moment Jesus Christ is setting you free to forgive.

Forgiveness can set you free. Whenever you have an ill feeling toward another person, you become that person's slave emotionally. Every place you go you take him with you. And the strangest phenomenon is that this emotional focus causes you to become just as bad as the person you resent, if not worse. You start out by saying, "I don't like that person," and you end up being worse.

In the September 1982 issue of *Guideposts* magazine, I read an article by Hasual Hanna of Aurora, Colorado. The story opened with these words, "If he'd done to your daughter what he did to mine, you probably would have hated him too."

The story goes on to describe how Mrs. Hanna's thirty-five-year-old daughter, Pat, was abducted in downtown Denver after work. She had been a beautiful Christian girl, had attended Bible college, and planned to be a missionary to reach people for Christ. A man called Carlton Moore raped her, stabbed her, and threw her out alongside the road, dead. The man was apprehended, tried, convicted, and sentenced.

In the story Mrs. Hanna tells about her bitterness, her hate for Carlton Moore. Her ill feelings consumed her. She withdrew from people, buried herself every day in her hate and grief. This miserable existence went on for two years.

Then something happened on a snowy Sunday in December 1971. She attended a Sunday school class in which Don Gentry of the local Gideons came and gave his testimony of how Bibles could be sent anywhere as a memorial for loved ones.

As he talked the Holy Spirit spoke to Mrs. Hanna's heart about planting a seed of love, being free of the miserable hatred she had lived in for so long.

The Holy Spirit talked to her about how God the Father lost His Son, Jesus, for our sins and forgiveness. She heard the Spirit of the Lord say to her, "Set yourself free by forgiving."

She prayed, "Dear Jesus, how can I forgive him, and mean it, with all this bitterness in my heart?"

Then came the words, "Have you forgotten My promise? If you forgive men their trespasses, your heavenly Father also will forgive you."

After class, she stepped forward and in an act of forgiveness and love asked Don Gentry to take the money she handed him and to send a Bible specifically to a convict named Carlton Moore. "Tell him, 'Because Jesus forgives her, Mrs. Hanna forgives you, and because Jesus said, "Love one another," Mrs. Hanna loves you!'"

As soon as she got home that day she fell across the bed and began to cry for the first time in years. After sobbing out all the pain and hurt, she realized that a miracle had happened. She was now set free.

Months later Don Gentry reported back to Mrs. Hanna that Carlton Moore received the Bible, and he accepted Jesus Christ. He was so moved by her act of love that it broke through his hardened heart and opened him up to God's forgiveness. Later Carlton Moore was to become a minister in the prison to fellow prisoners.

Yes, forgiveness can set you free. Forgiving others through the power of Christ within you will work the miracle of renewal in your relationships.

As you practice these principles and do everything you can to reach out to others in love, you will have the fulfillment of knowing that you are living the way Christ wants you to live. Added to that, you will enjoy some wonderful, lasting relationships.

IN A CAPSULE

• Principle 1 •

Be a peacemaker.

• **Principle 2** •

Work out your anger quickly.

• **Principle 3** •

Speak the truth in love.

• **Principle 4** •

*There are no enduring relationships
without forgiveness.*

 PART II

Getting Along with Difficult People

4

Recognize the Irregulars

*Eight types of difficult people and
how to successfully cope with them*

Any intelligent human being should be able to
get along with everyone. Right? No, wrong!
Many fine, intelligent persons have a tough
time getting along with irregular people. Well, if
you're not only intelligent but well adjusted in your
personality, enjoying a high degree of self-esteem,
then you should be able to get along well with anyone
and everyone. Right? No, we need not look far to
find an intelligent, well-adjusted person, with a high
degree of self-esteem, who continues to struggle in
a relationship with what I call "a difficult person."

I heard a preacher say, "If you're a citizen of the Kingdom of God, then you will have right relationships with everyone in your life." Is this true? Reality is that in everyday life, it doesn't work out that way. Some of the finest Christian people I know have trouble getting along with difficult persons.

Three cheers for my friend Joyce Landorf, who in her book *Irregular People* had the openness and honesty to share the pain inflicted upon her by the irregular person in her life. She described this person as having been harsh in his criticism toward her, unaccepting of her person, and totally blinded to her emotional needs. This beautiful Christian lady who had achieved so much had been unable to win the approval and recognition that she craved from this irregular family member. By Joyce's own admission, across the years she had tried every conceivable approach to try to relate well to him; yet all had failed. It seemed that the harder she tried to relate to him, the more pain and rejection she suffered.

I want to help you with that difficult person in your life. It may be a member of your immediate family. Possibly it's your boss. Or if you are a boss, maybe an employee gets under your skin. It may be a neighbor or a person at church. Just about everyone faces some difficult person. A saying tells us, "A frog has a wonderful advantage in life—he can eat everything that bugs him." Now I am going to help you to cope with the people who bug you.

Who Is *Difficult*

We all have days when we're not pleasant to get along with, but if you contact someone who *consistently* acts sneaky, hostile, negative, and unresponsive to others' needs, you know a difficult person.

Such a man will cause problems for those around him, and normal kinds of communication fail to reach him. Accepting responsibility for what goes wrong will never be his strong point, nor will he want to repent of any wrongdoing on his part. He will not ask for forgiveness or apologize. In short, the difficult person is a heartbreaker.

Because someone rubs you the wrong way does not mean he or she is a difficult person. Perhaps your personalities clash. Some people just do not bring out the best in each other. It is a combination of the way each of them is wired. They just don't match up right.

But doesn't the Bible teach us that we must get along with everyone? Where in the Bible does it say that? Now, it *does* tell us we are to *love* everyone. But does that mean that we are going to be on excellent terms with everyone? Will we share close friendships with everyone? Does it mean we should only encounter relationships free from stress and conflict?

In Romans 12:18 we read these words: "If it be possible, as much as lieth in you, live peaceably with all men." What is this verse teaching? To me it says, "Do the best you can to get along with everyone. But also realize that once in a while you are going to have a relationship with a difficult person, and it is going to fall short of being ideal."

To help you develop your understanding and your strategies for dealing with difficult people, I share with you:

Eight Types of Difficult People and Strategies for Success

Type 1: The Sherman Tank. According to Robert M. Bramson in *Coping with Difficult People*, this describes the aggressive, often hostile person who tries to roll right over others. He is an expert on anything and everything. "I am right, and you are wrong," his attitude cries. This aggressive, pushy, manipulating person may victimize you and then turn around and make you feel like a crook.

How do you handle the Sherman Tank? Your basic strategy has to be: "I am not going to allow this person to run me over." You don't have to fight him, but you must practice this principle:

• Principle 1 •
Stand up for yourself.

A businessman who for years had cheated on his taxes, to the tune of several hundred thousand dollars, was convicted and sent to prison. The church of which he was a member stood by him and his family and supported them as much as possible.

Following the man's release from prison, he was faced with a judgment to make restitution for the money he had stolen. The man went to see the pastor and the church administrator and attempted to steamroll them. He wanted the church leaders to assume responsibility to pay back all the money he had taken. The business administrator later described this as a strange phenomenon when he said, "There we were, listening to the man who had committed the crime and feeling as if we were the criminals."

How did the leaders of the church handle the Sherman Tank? To the business manager's credit, he stood up and told the man in no uncertain terms that the church was not responsible for his sin and could in no way take over his responsibilities to pay back the debt.

Once the man was confronted by the straightforward truth, the manipulation game ended. Before this, he stirred up a lot of trouble among the members. But once stood up to, he disappeared from the fellowship of the church.

If you do not stand up for yourself with a Sherman Tank, you will get run over. If you allow a Sherman Tank to run over you, you will be angry with yourself. The Sherman Tank only respects the person who has the courage and the audacity to stand up to him.

Type 2: The Space Cadet. A Space Cadet acts and thinks as if he were from a different planet. You can talk until you're blue in the face, but he doesn't hear you. If you expect some emotional response from this person, you are going to be hurt all the more, because you're not going to receive it. This difficult person lives in his own world and does only what he wants to do.

There are people, both Christians and non-Christians, who simply operate on a different wavelength. For the most part they act as if they were from Mars. They park where they're not supposed to park. They show up where they don't belong. They take charge when they're not supposed to be in charge.

How do you handle and get along with a Space Cadet? The first thing to do is make up your mind that you will not allow the Space Cadet in your life to drive you bonkers. But how do you do that? By practicing this principle:

• Principle 2 •

Accept him as being from a different planet.

To accept a person as being a Space Cadet means recognizing that he or she has always been like that, and no matter what you do or say he or she is still going to be like that. So why spin your tires and burn up your rubber trying to change what can't be changed? You're not responsible for another's actions and attitudes anyway.

Type 3: The Volcano. Difficult people of the Volcano type are either exploding or building up steam, getting ready to explode. Usually family members and other people who have to live with them walk around on pins and needles, never knowing when another eruption is coming. Volcanoes often get their own way by intimidating others. Wherever they are, they generate a feeling of tension.

One of the most recognizable faces in Portland, Oregon, is businessman Tom Peterson. You cannot read the *TV Guide*, pick up the newspaper, or long watch television without seeing Tom in his commercials. Tom belongs to our New Hope Community Church. He is gifted, hardworking, and a pacesetter in marketing television sets, stereo and video equipment, and other home furnishings.

One day I asked Tom what he does with a guy who has bought a new color television set to watch the Super Bowl game and returns the next day like a raging bull because right in the middle of the game the set went on the blink. What do you do with an irate customer who erupts like a volcano?

Tom smiled and shared with me: "I stand there and listen. Sometimes I listen for a long time without saying a word, except to agree with what the person is saying. I give him the time to run down. When he has gotten it pretty well out, I ask him to tell me the story one more time, so I am sure I understand it. The next time through he usually talks in normal voice tones." The Bible gives us this age-old principle for dealing with the Volcano:

• Principle 3 •

"A soft answer turneth away wrath."

Proverbs 15:1

Type 4: The Spoiler. He complains chronically. No matter what happens, the Spoiler still grumbles and acts negative. For example, a woman griped because she lived in a little, rented apartment. Now she lives in a luxurious, ten-room house in one of the finest sections of the city, and she's still complaining. If you asked her to write down all her objections and tomorrow proceeded to eliminate every one, before you could get through her odd list, she would have a new one.

You cannot satisfy the Spoiler because he never feels satisfied with himself. If your father fits in this category, you have learned that no matter what you do, he won't seem pleased. So what do you do? Recognize this difficult person for being a Spoiler. To cope with him, you cannot allow him to squeeze you into his way of negative thinking. You do not want his perspective on life to become yours. Instead:

• **Principle 4** •

Choose and cultivate your own
positive mental attitude.

The Spoiler should not do your thinking for you. If you allow him to, you will lose your perspective and become negative yourself.

Pick out any successful ministry where people are being won to Jesus, people are being healed, and lives are being put back together through the power of God, and inside every one you will find some Spoiler types. Thousands of people may be helped, yet all he sees is negative. He locks himself into the negative by choosing to think and dwell on what's wrong instead of what's right.

Whether or not the Spoiler in your life ever understands and practices this Bible verse, make sure you do, and you will have victory. "Fix your thoughts on what is true and good and right. Think about things that are pure and lovely, and dwell on the fine, good things in others. Think about all you can praise God for and be glad about" (Phil. 4:8 TLB).

Notice the word *fix*. No matter what the Spoiler is saying, the choice of what you think is yours. You still have the power within your mind to choose and select what you will think. Instead of magnifying what's wrong, by the power of your own choice decide to think on the positive and in gratitude praise God for it. The positive choice is always your best choice.

Now notice the word *dwell* in Philippians 4:8. To *dwell* means that you keep your mind centered on the positive. You concentrate on it. You work at developing the habit of thinking positive. Take charge of your own thinking and refuse to surrender the control of your mind to the Spoiler. You will gain altitude with a positive attitude.

Type 5: The Wet Blanket. This difficult person is the classic impossibility thinker. No matter what is proposed, he automatically responds, "It can't be done."

"It won't work." "It's never been done before." "It's impossible."

I had a friend who worked in counseling with a woman who was a Wet Blanket. He told me that he spent hundreds of hours trying to get the woman off dead center and motivated to do something to help herself. But no matter what he suggested she do to get off welfare and get a job, her automatic response was, "It won't work, it's impossible." My friend told me that one day he gave her a list of twenty-five things that she could do to improve her miserable state in life. Guess what? She had twenty-five reasons why none of those suggestions would work. In a few minutes she shot down every possibility. This Wet Blanket had made it a habit to be an impossibility thinker, and in so doing, locked herself into continuing to be the helpless victim.

How do you get along with a difficult person who's a Wet Blanket? For starters, don't put one on your church board. Don't expect one to support a great idea. And most of all, don't allow one to dampen your enthusiasm for life. Your strategy for getting along with a Wet Blanket is to allow him the right to be an impossibility thinker, while not surrendering any leadership to him. Do this by practicing this principle in your own life:

• **Principle 5** •

Be a possibility thinker.

Type 6: The Garbage Collector. Garbage Collectors are actually worse off than the Spoiler and Wet Blanket, because they are locked even deeper into the mire of the negative. They have surrendered the leadership of their lives to negative emotions. Oh, how they love to rehearse and replay the injuries they have suffered at the hands of other people. They nurse their wounds and hold on to their wounded ill spirit.

Almost every Christian organization has its human Garbage Collectors, people so emotionally hypnotized with their own sick feelings that they relate to everything around them from this emotional illness.

This type maintains a cover, often thin and transparent, from behind which, like a sniper, they take potshots at you. As Robert M. Bramson, in his book *Coping with Difficult People*, says, "Their weapons are rocks hidden in snowballs: innuendoes, *sotto voce* remarks, not-too-subtle digs, non-playful teasing, and the like."

How do you handle a human Garbage Collector who accepts the negative like manure and spreads it around, stinking up everything? The first thing you do is pray a lot for him and try to be God's servant in bringing the healing and change he needs in his life. If he refuses to change and persists in harming other people, however, you will need to directly confront him about his disruptive behavior.

Understand that Garbage Collectors are basically cowards. They fear confronting their ill feelings, and telling other people face-to-face what they really think. So the strategy is to confront them, in front of other mature people, with what they have been implying or saying behind your back. You do this by asking them direct questions and holding them to an answer. For example, "Is this how you feel?" "Is this what you'd like to say?" "Do you believe this, or don't you?" You have to pin them down and not let them squirm out of it. You smoke them out. The principle you want to practice is this:

• Principle 6 •

Never surrender leadership to another
person's negative and ill emotions.

Type 7: The User. These difficult types are the alcoholics, drug addicts, gambling addicts, emotionally dependent, and spoiled children. They will do anything to manipulate you into providing what they want when they want it. If you're not careful, they will make you their slaves by putting you on a guilt trip. The user takes no responsibility for himself, but wants you to carry all his responsibilities.

How do you get along with a User? Be firm in the application of this tough-love principle:

• Principle 7 •

You set the limits.

Most people are probably too reluctant in going to their pastor for counsel in times of need. But it takes only one or two demanding Users to completely deplete the emotional energies of a pastor, Christian worker, or anyone else who deals with people. The User demands everything—full attention—and refuses to do anything to help himself.

I'll never forget my first pastoral-ministry experience with a User. This particular lady drove the pastor that preceded me into the idea of moving to another church just to get away. I hadn't been in town a week when she started calling me every day, talking for two or three hours, whining on and on. I soon discovered that she would do nothing for herself to try to change where she was. All she wanted was to use me for her daily emotional dumping ground. In the process she was depleting all my emotional energy. I had nothing left to give to the many other people in the congregation.

After about a month of this, I got smart and set some limits. I told her, "Now, I'm concerned about you, and I want to help you, but here are the limits. You may call me every Friday morning at 9:30, and we will talk for fifteen minutes, and that's it." That kept me from being used and abused.

Some parents are being victimized by children who have become users and abusers. The only way to get along with such a difficult child is to set some limits.

Type 8: The Emotionally Handicapped. There exist persons who have been so deeply wounded emotionally that they have developed a handicap when it comes to relating to others. Such people may, in their behavior, ignore others, or they may go to the other extreme and attack. You may bear the brunt of these actions. Or you may find that when you are loving and kind, they just don't respond. Somehow you need to look beyond the unsatisfying behavior and see the pain in the eyes of these people and the wounding in their spirits. Often difficult people are simply good people who have been battered and scarred emotionally.

They need healing. In this Jesus calls us to be His agents, one to another (see James 5:16).

In Luke's Gospel, the tenth chapter, in response to a question, "Who is my neighbor?" Jesus told the parable of the Good Samaritan: A man falls among abusers and is victimized. He is beaten, bruised, and left to die. The first two men who come his way pass him by and leave him bleeding in his pain and suffering. But the third man, a Samaritan, stops and in compassion and love ministers to the man's wounds. He picks him up and puts him on his own beast, takes him into the town, and pays for his care and recovery.

What is the central lesson Jesus wants to teach us? It is this: Be compassionate to the wounded, however they have suffered it.

God's principle concerning the emotionally handicapped is:

• Principle 8 •

Be compassionate and loving to the emotionally wounded, and you will see miracles of healing.

Did you know that even a cat that has been wounded emotionally responds to love?

I personally didn't like cats. Probably because I'd never been around them much. They always seemed a little bit sneaky to me. Margi, when she was being brought up, always had a kitten or cat, and she really likes cats. Well, throughout our married life she worked on me to have a cat, and I said no. But then she found a way. She planted the thought in the mind of our daughter Ann.

When Ann was four years of age, she started asking me just about every day, "Daddy, could I have a little kitty?" Well, I really couldn't find it in my heart to say no and didn't want to say yes, so I'd just smile. Then she started praying every night, asking God for a little kitty.

After about a month of this praying, one evening there came to our back door (which meant it had to somehow get through the fence) this cute little orange kitten with white around its nose and down underneath its neck. Margi announced to Ann, "There's your kitten! Here, quick, take it some milk."

Ann was saying, "God answered my prayer. I got my kitten."

Now, what was I going to do? I had been had! So that's how we got Fluffy at our house.

About the first year and a half or two years, by all standards, Fluffy was a weird cat. Readers who love kittens or cats are probably thinking, *Well, he just doesn't like cats. That's why he's saying that.* But even Margi, a real lover of cats, agreed that this was a pretty strange one.

Fluffy would not let you pet him. When our kids tried to play with him, he ended up scratching them. I don't know how many times Ann came in, crying, with scratches. And when people would come to our house, that cat would go into orbit. You could just see the fear in his eyes. We decided he must have been terribly abused the four or five months before he came to live at our house.

As soon as the kitten was old enough to be a cat, we got him fixed, thinking that would tame his wild temperament. For months afterwards, it didn't seem to make any difference. He was still a cold, unresponsive, fear-ridden cat.

About this time, I wanted in the worst way to get rid of Fluffy, but Margi and Ann would not give up on him. He got into a fight with a neighborhood cat and got all torn up. We had to take him to the vet. Here I was, spending money on a worthless cat. I figured God had sent this cat to us to teach me tolerance. Various family members tried to hold Fluffy or pet him. About all they got were negative reactions.

Finally Fluffy started to warm up to Margi a little bit, but still wouldn't have anything to do with me or Ann. Next Fluffy warmed up to Ann; she finally broke through to him.

After almost four years of living together, I still have a problem with Fluffy, but it's a different one. Every morning, while I'm shaving, he comes in and keeps rubbing himself against my bare legs, wanting my love and attention. I sit down at night, and he jumps up in the chair beside me. He's warmed up to me, a person who didn't like cats.

Our TLC group comes to the house, and he doesn't even get upset. That fear in his eyes vanished. Now if love can transform a disturbed cat into a peaceful one, what do you think love can do for the emotionally wounded and scarred human? Love, when it is patient; love, when it goes the second mile; love, when it gives without thought of return; love, when it's God's kind of love, is the one thing that heals.

Let God's love and the wisdom gained from studying these types be yours in getting along with the persons in your life. Having identified the eight types of difficult people, in the next chapter I will share with you eight universal principles for getting along with all types of difficult persons.

.... **IN A CAPSULE** ....

● **Principle 1** ●
Stand up for yourself.

● **Principle 2** ●
Accept him as being from a different planet.

● **Principle 3** ●
"A soft answer turneth away wrath."
Proverbs 15:1

• **Principle 4** •

*Choose and cultivate your own
positive mental attitude.*

• **Principle 5** •

Be a possibility thinker.

• **Principle 6** •

*Never surrender leadership to another
person's negative and ill emotions.*

• **Principle 7** •

You set the limits.

• **Principle 8** •

*Be compassionate and loving to the emotionally
wounded, and you will see miracles of healing.*

5

Counterattack with Positive Actions

Eight universal principles for getting along with difficult folk

A Texan died and went to his reward. Once inside the gate, he stood there, taking it all in. The host came to escort him to his eternal abode.

The Texan turned to the host and said, "Pardner, I didn't realize that heaven was so much like Texas."

The host replied, "Man, you aren't in heaven."

When you continually have to deal with the same difficult person in your everyday life, you know that you are not in heaven. It challenges all the skills and self-control you can muster.

In order to carry out the Golden Rule principle, "Treat others as you want to be treated," in such a situation, you must learn to initiate right actions instead of merely reacting to what other people do or do not do. Jesus taught us that we are not to live as children of darkness in this world, but as children of light, citizens of the Kingdom of God, who intentionally initiate right actions toward others.

When it comes to getting along with people, and particularly difficult people, Jesus is our guide and example. Considering all the difficult people Jesus had to deal with, it's a wonder that He kept His sanity. They made Him out to be a troublemaker when He was a peacemaker. The Man of Love was constantly the object of the hatred of difficult people. Jesus felt their ingratitude, misunderstanding, rejection, and betrayal. When you study Jesus' life and realize all the abusive treatment He suffered from irregular people, you marvel that He didn't become disturbed Himself.

Yet not once did He allow another's bizarre behavior to dictate what He would do. Neither did He allow all the misbehavior directed at Him to change His spirit from one of love. Jesus did not allow anyone to sidetrack Him from the will of the Father. What enormous strength and self-control He exhibited.

In the Bible we read these words: "In the world ye shall have tribulation: but be of good cheer; I have overcome the world" (John 16:33). When we feel overrun and under attack from the misbehavior of a difficult person in our lives, we need to move close to Jesus and draw our strength and direction from Him. Remember, "Greater is he that is in you, than he that is in the world" (1 John 4:4).

Deal with Difficult People by Counterattacking with Positive Actions

How do you counterattack with positive actions? The Bible tells us, "Don't let evil get the upper hand but conquer evil by doing good" (Rom. 12:21 TLB). In facing the difficult person or persons in your life, you can overcome evil by doing good; counterattack with positive action by learning and using these principles:

Eight Universal Principles for Getting Along with Difficult Folk

• Principle 1 •
Be confident in who you are.

Confidence in who you are forms the basis for good self-esteem. When relating to a difficult person, remember that your worth does not depend upon that person's opinion of you. Your worth as a person comes as a gift from God.

A while back a lady who I would consider a troubled and difficult person blamed me for everything bad that was going on in her life. This disturbed woman was saying, in effect, "You told me to do this, and then you told me to do that. Therefore, everything is your fault."

I replied, "Hey, wait a minute, I've never made it a practice in my entire ministry to tell people what to do. I've spent countless hours helping them to look at all the alternatives. I've done what I could to help them make right decisions. But it never has been and never will be my style to make people's decisions for them."

You see, I could stand up to this woman who was distorting the truth because I knew who I was, a child of God, and I knew the principles that I use in counseling with people.

One of the characteristics of difficult people is that they do blame others and heap abuse on them. When this happens, we must be on guard, because as Stanley C. Baldwin says in his book, *A True View of You*, "When people give us negative feedback we tend to internalize that and think or feel badly about ourselves." So what we have to do is refuse by an act of our own will to accept a difficult person's warped view of us. In other words, do not allow a disturbed, maladjusted person to make you feel crummy about yourself.

How do you do this? By remembering that God, your heavenly Father, gave you worth at birth. Whatever of that worth was lost by sin has been restored in your second birth, the spiritual birth. I love the phrase in Ephesians 1:6 that tells me that I am "accepted in the beloved."

• Principle 2 •

Don't allow yourself to overreact.

A funny thing happened in Darlington, Maryland, several years ago. Edith, a mother of eight children, was coming home from visiting a neighbor one Saturday afternoon. As she walked into the house, she spotted five of her youngest children huddled together, concentrating with intense interest on something. When she slipped over near them, trying to discover what was going on, she could hardly believe her eyes. Smack-dab in the middle of the circle of attention were several baby skunks.

The alarmed mother screamed at the top of her voice, "Children, run, run, run!" At the sound of her voice, each kid grabbed a skunk and ran. You can picture what happened next!

Panicking, screaming, and overreacting are not the way to handle skunks. Neither do they help in handling a difficult person. You cannot allow another's difficult behavior to consume your life. Avoid that by refusing to overreact. Restrain yourself from allowing the situation to be blown all out of proportion.

If you find yourself reacting negatively to everything he does, then you're probably overreacting.

Even the most difficult person usually has some good attributes and behavior.

• Principle 3 •

Refuse to play the difficult person's games.

Judas was one of the chosen twelve disciples that Jesus took into His confidence and inner circle. Jesus gave Judas His time and trust and poured His life and teachings into him. Added to this, He gave that disciple the same complete, unconditional love He gave to the other chosen ones. Yet Judas betrayed Jesus for thirty pieces of silver. Judas was certainly a difficult person. Yet knowing full well what Judas had done, Jesus showed love to Judas by washing his dirty feet, sharing food with him, and giving him an honored place at the table (see John 13). Jesus, who was in control of Himself, refused to play Judas's kind of destructive game.

Difficult people, by their very behavior, try to manipulate us or gain control over us. Their variety of games is endless and can consume an enormous amount of time and energy. Simply refuse to play the game. You do have a choice. Just exercise that power.

Any person in authority over other people takes some abuse for being in that position. The larger the responsibility, the more abuse he receives. My own father, a very successful administrator over 140 churches in Ohio for thirty years, refused to play the difficult person's game.

In my adult life I was surprised to learn of two pastors in Dad's district who for years created a small pocket of opposition to his leadership. I was five years of age when Dad first became a district superintendent. In all my boyhood and teen years I never once heard him say anything derogatory about either of these men. In fact, when they got into difficulty in their local churches, my father, knowing full well that they had voted against his continuation as district leader, went to bat for them in seeing that they were placed in new pastorates at different churches. Dad's way to face destructive behavior directed at him was to overcome it by doing good. This is exactly what, as Christians, Jesus asks us to do.

• Principle 4 •

When you need to confront,
do it immediately.

In chapter three we talked about caring enough to confront as one of the key principles in lasting relationships. When you deal with a difficult person, this becomes even more urgent, but aims at a different goal. Now you struggle to get through the best way you can. By facing up to the person, you forestall his taking charge. If you fail to do so immediately, his misbehavior could overrun you.

There's always a strong temptation to put off the unpleasant. You don't even want to be around the problem person, let alone hit him with truth. But putting it off only makes things worse. The sooner you stand up to him, the better off you are going to be.

When dealing with an irregular person, do not allow yourself to be caught up in detailed argument about who's right and who's wrong. That's a game; don't play it. Simply invite him to express his viewpoint. Then ask him to listen to your thoughts on the subject. State your opinion and position clearly and firmly.

The target is better understanding, but since difficult people hardly see anything except from their own viewpoint, do not be disappointed if they do not fully accept what you're saying. Just the fact that you have backed them off or stopped some of their abusive behavior is itself not a small victory.

• Principle 5 •

Have realistic expectations.

One of the biggest mistakes we make in trying to relate to these persons in our lives, especially those whom we have to relate to regularly, is to expect more from them emotionally than they are able to give.

Joyce Landorf, in her book *Irregular People*, shares a letter written to her by her dear friend and famous author Dr. James Dobson. This letter was a kind response to his friend Joyce, who was hurting from the blows suffered at the hand of her difficult person.

Your irregular person never met the needs that he should have satisfied earlier in your life, and I think you are still hoping he will miraculously become what he has never been. Therefore, he constantly disappoints you—hurts you and rejects you.

I think you will be less vulnerable to pain when you accept the fact that he cannot, nor will he ever, provide the love and empathy and interest that he should. It is not easy to insulate yourself in this way . . . but it hurts less to expect nothing than to hope in vain.

I would guess that your irregular person's own childhood experiences account for his emotional peculiarities, and can perhaps be viewed as his own unique handicap. If he were blind, you would love him despite his lack of vision. In a sense, he is emotionally "blind." He's blind to your needs. He's unaware of the hurts behind the incidents and the disinterest in your accomplishments, and now Rick's wedding. His handicap makes it impossible for him to perceive your feelings and anticipation. If you can accept him as a man with a permanent handicap—one which was probably caused when he was vulnerable—you will shield yourself from the ice pick of his rejection.[1]

Wounded birds can't fly. And hurting people can't give out much love. Understand this, and stop having unrealistic expectations. Face it, they're not capable of giving you what you need. So why set yourself up to be hurt when you don't have to be hurt anymore?

1. Joyce Landorf, *Irregular People* (Waco, Tex.: Word Books, 1982), 61–62. Used by permission.

By changing your expectations to more realistic ones, you can save yourself a lot of pain and rejection.

• Principle 6 •

Stop trying to change the difficult person in your life.

We have learned that unconditional acceptance is important in any relationship. But when it comes to difficult persons, principle six, based on unconditional love, becomes a lifesaver.

Trying to change anyone against his will brings only heartbreak. Yet when you have to deal with a problem person on a regular basis, your need to change him may become tense and urgent. *If somehow I could change him*, you may think, *it would relieve all this trouble.*

No matter how urgent your need becomes, you must resist the temptation. This wrong approach cannot change him. He can only change himself. If you persist in trying to change him, what you will do is create more tension, frustration, and trouble for yourself in the relationship.

James Stewart's classic book, *The Life and Teachings of Jesus Christ*, says of Jesus' teachings, although they were authoritarian, "it was never in any overbearing sense didactic or dogmatic or forcing assent." In other words, Jesus respected the right of the individual to make his own choices. God even allows man the freedom to commit the worst of sins. That's how much God respects the human will.

Sometimes we must come to a point where we stop being responsible for other people's behavior. We must accept the fact that until they choose to act differently, they are going to keep on being the same old difficult persons. Do yourself a big favor and avoid a lot of internal tension by just accepting people as they are.

• Principle 7 •

Keep yourself from being the difficult person's slave.

This principle is particularly useful when dealing with the User or the Sherman Tank, where you can easily become a slave to the other person's dominant, assertive, and abrasive personality. When I was a young pastor in my first church, one abrasive User-type woman had me running errands for her. I ran to the grocery store for her. I took her kids to the doctor. The last straw was when she called me to take her pet to the veterinarian. That was when I finally stood up and said, "No, I'm not going to be used anymore."

In trying to relate to abrasive, manipulative people, refuse to allow them to control your life. When they try to put you on the guilt trip because you're not doing what they want you to do, remember that you still have a choice. By an act of your own will refuse to take the guilt trip. When they try to make you responsible for their debts, troubles, or woes, you have a choice. No matter what they're telling you, you don't have to accept what they're saying. You do not have to take on their responsibilities. The only way to relate to a difficult person who is trying to make you do what you don't want to do is to stand up and say no.

In dealing with that problem person, keep some distance between yourself and the manipulation. Sometimes you have to take two steps away and detach yourself enough to see what's happening.

If you do not assert yourself with a difficult person, you will become his slave and dislike yourself for it. So when you need to, stand up for yourself. If the difficult person does not respect you for it, at least he will back off enough to give you the breathing room you need.

• **Principle 8** •

*Let God lead you through your struggle
with that difficult person.*

We must be careful not to allow a difficult person's destructive behavior to so disturb us that it robs us of our inner peace. Amazingly one disturbed person can create an atmosphere of fear and havoc in the lives of those around him.

What do you do when someone in your life causes a big disturbance? The miracle story recorded in John 6:16–21 has always been one of my favorites. The disciples, people like ourselves, were caught in an uncontrollable storm. The lake churned, and the waves rolled. Their boat was being tossed in the storm and they felt afraid. Sometimes we get involved in a stormy disturbance started by another. We cannot allow fear to take over in our lives.

In the midst of that kind of storm, we need to see Jesus. Just when the disciples needed Him the most, He came walking on the troubled waters and calmed not only the water but the fears in their hearts. Jesus spoke and said, "It is I; be not afraid" (John 6:20). In the midst of your disturbance, see Jesus and hear Him say, "It is I; be not afraid."

Every time we turn our eyes on Jesus and ask for His help, a peace comes from Him into our hearts. The Bible says, "And the peace of God, which passeth all understanding, shall keep your hearts and minds through Christ Jesus" (Phil. 4:7).

Joseph, a favorite Old Testament character, suffered more at the hands of difficult people than almost anyone else I know, except for Jesus Christ. Joseph's insanely jealous brothers sold him into slavery. That is being victimized by destructive behavior. As if that weren't enough, once he had worked himself up into a trusted position in Potiphar's house, Potiphar's sensual witch of a wife falsely accused Joseph. This resulted in his confinement in prison for seven years.

Joseph didn't have just one difficult person in his life. He didn't have just two in his life. He had ten irregular brothers, who conspired to kill him, and a sinful woman, who lied about him. Yet with all this and with the passing of many years before he was to be vindicated, Joseph still kept his life surrendered to the leadership of God. He trusted his most difficult relationships to the direction and vindication of God. How powerful are Joseph's words when, after he revealed himself to his brothers, he said from his heart, "You meant evil against me; but God meant it for good" (Gen. 50:20 RSV). Somewhere along the line Joseph accepted his difficult brothers as they were, trusting the outcome of the entire relationship to God.

God expects us to live under His control and leadership, not under the power of that difficult person. As we follow the Lord, we have the promise that He'll not only bring us through the struggle, but if we are obedient children, He will bring us out on top, the victor: "And we know that all things work together for good to them that love God, to them who are the called according to his purpose" (Rom. 8:28).

·············· **IN A CAPSULE** ··············

• Principle 1 •
Be confident in who you are.

• Principle 2 •
Don't allow yourself to overreact.

• Principle 3 •
Refuse to play the difficult person's games.

• Principle 4 •
When you need to confront, do it immediately.

• Principle 5 •

Have realistic expectations.

• Principle 6 •

Stop trying to change the difficult person in your life.

• Principle 7 •

Keep yourself from being the difficult person's slave.

• Principle 8 •

*Let God lead you through your struggle
with that difficult person.*

6

The Art of Turning the Other Cheek

*Five principles to help you handle
abusive treatment*

As we live in relationships, sooner or later we are going to face some sort of abusive treatment. This may come from a difficult person, or it may come from a casual friend or even someone close. From time to time it happens. And when it does, you're holding a hot potato.

What do you do when you're a professional baseball player, and after twenty years of being the most productive hitter on the team, you come to the plate on opening day, 1982, and 70,000 ungrateful fans heap their abuse on you by booing? That's what happened to Andre Thornton of the Cleveland Indians. By his own admission it was very difficult to take. The year before, Andre had been plagued by injuries. Previous to opening day, the Cleveland papers had pitted a younger, more popular player against the veteran. They implied that Thornton was over the hill and that the rookie should be playing.

Before opening day Andre and his wife, anticipating some of the problems that he would be facing in a comeback, sought guidance from the Lord. As they prayed together, asking the Lord for help, they received assurance that God would give them the strength to stand true and not strike back. They also received a promise from the Lord that He would vindicate Andre and use this opposition to bring glory to God.

Following the humiliating experience on opening day, as the season unfolded, Andre Thornton made one of baseball's spectacular comebacks. Even greater than the comeback was his witness and impact for Christ in Cleveland and in other baseball cities. By turning the other cheek and refusing to react to mistreatment, Andre found many doors open to speak for his Lord.

What do you do when you are abused and mistreated? What do you do when you are a leader and someone lies about you and attacks your leadership?

What do you do when a best friend turns against you and hurls abusive treatment at you? Well, acting naturally, you will retaliate and compound the injuries. Apart from the presence, power, and principles of Jesus, people always have and still continue to live this destructive way: "An eye for an eye, and a tooth for a tooth" (Matt. 5:38).

Jesus came to teach us and show us a better way to live and to relate.

No one has ever suffered more from the consequences of other people's sins than Jesus. The Pure One, the Perfect One, the compassionate Jesus, who never showed anything but love toward other people, was treated more unjustly than anyone who has ever lived.

Jesus was the victim of the cruelest of emotional insults as well as physical pain. He was rejected by His own people, lied against by religious leaders, betrayed by one of His own disciples, misunderstood by His mother and brothers and sisters.

The One who did not deserve any ill treatment was blasphemed, ridiculed, laughed at, and scorned. Finally He was convicted and sentenced to death on false charges and given a bum rap. The final insult was being cursed and crucified on a cross.

Note this: Not once did He lose His cool. Not once did He react to ill treatment with worse actions. Not once did He strike back. Such enormous self-control and inner strength and love the world has never seen, except in Jesus.

Jesus, the Son of God, Was Never a Reactor but Always a Responder

Jesus is our perfect example, the leader among men. He came giving us a better way to relate and live with one another in peace.

In the Sermon on the Mount, Jesus said, "The law of Moses says, 'If a man gouges out another's eye, he must pay with his own eye. If a tooth gets knocked out, knock out the tooth of the one who did it.' But I say: Don't resist violence! If you are slapped on one cheek, turn the other too" (Matt. 5:38, 39 TLB).

"Turning the other cheek" is an advanced step in our Golden Rule principle. It means that no matter how badly you may be treated by others, you do not react with the same abuse. Despite the temptation to lash back, you don't do it. You do not seek vengeance, neither do you retaliate.

"Turning the other cheek" means so much more than physically turning the other cheek so someone can slap you again on the other side. It means keeping control of your own emotions and your responses. It means refusing to give the devil any foothold in your life.

I have already said that we sometimes have to stand up to difficult people who abuse us. I am not saying now to forget all about that and passively accept mistreatment. A continuing challenge of the Christian life, however, is to live not for ourselves alone, but for Christ and others. When we are abused, this is especially difficult. Instead of being overly concerned with self-vindication, we must learn to trust Jesus to vindicate us.

Let's face it, "turning the other cheek" is not easy. Often the easy thing to do would be to throw the punch, to strike back. In our own power we will want to claim our rights, set the record straight, show that so-and-so he can't get by with mistreating us.

When it comes to learning and mastering this difficult art, we need the Holy Spirit to be our helper. Without His power we cannot practice these principles for handling abusive treatment:

Five Principles to Help You Handle Abusive Treatment

Like it or not, we all receive such treatment in life; no one avoids it. In a world of imperfect people and many choices, who among us will do everything right all the time? And even if we did, some critic would find fault with it all.

Things Aren't Fair. When things don't go their way, children frequently use the line "It's not fair!" As equitable as parents try to be, their sibling rivals still voice such complaints.

This desire for equality doesn't die with age. *Everyone* wants to be treated justly and fairly. But that doesn't always happen. Ours is an unjust, unfair world, because of the sin that exists on earth. Good people often suffer undeservedly. Principle one reflects the only way to deal with that truth:

• Principle 1 •

Accept the reality of unfairness.

As we relate to other people, we discover that most are out to protect their own interests. They think of themselves first, and whether or not that's the way it should be, that's the way it is. So why should we waste our breath muttering things like, "I can't believe the way people act"?

As you relate to others, sometimes you'll be misunderstood. At other times, someone will take his anger out on you. On other occasions, a person says something unfair or untrue about you. From time to time you are going to be the target of abusive treatment.

When you receive unjust treatment, what do you do about it? Sit around and feel sorry for yourself? Self-pity is the one luxury you cannot afford. That just makes matters worse. As a first step in handling such treatment, accept the reality of unfairness. Stop struggling. That doesn't mean you like it. It does mean that you recognize you cannot change or be responsible for other people's misbehavior. Determine that you are not going to allow it to get you down.

As a Christian, you will at times be mistreated because you follow Jesus. Just when you are trying your best to do what's right, someone will attack you because you believe in Him. Listen to what Jesus says to us: "Happy are those who are persecuted because they are good, for the Kingdom of Heaven is theirs. When you are reviled and persecuted and lied about because you are my followers—wonderful! Be happy about it! Be very glad! For a tremendous reward awaits you up in heaven. And remember, the ancient prophets were persecuted too" (Matt. 5:10–12 TLB).

Whenever we are treated unjustly or unfairly, remember that we live not only in the present but in preparation for eternity. Then Our Father will straighten everything out. In light of this, can we not accept the present reality of unfairness?

How Do You React? When someone strikes you or attacks you, the most natural instinct is to retaliate. But let's stop and think that through a moment. Someone hurts you, so you hurt him. So he hurts you, and you hurt him again. In this way wars escalate. No problem in human relationships can be solved by striking back. To the contrary, destruction occurs when people give in to their lower urges and seek vengeance.

In *Ben Hur*, the central character, Judah Ben Hur, returns to Israel intent on one thing: revenge. Because of one man's mistreatment, he has wasted years of his young manhood away in the galley of a slave ship. Ben Hur's historic position and fortune have been desolated. Because of this same enemy, his mother and sister are rotting away as lepers in a cave outside Jerusalem.

Judah lives to avenge himself. To bring Messala down into the dirt becomes his driving motive. This passion so consumes Ben Hur that his beloved, Esther, looking into his tortured eyes, exclaims, "Judah Ben Hur, you have become a Messala."

When you are set on making the other person pay for his actions, you become as bad as or worse than that person. No matter how unjustly someone treats you, that does not give you the right to retaliate. Realize that in this world you are going to receive some mistreatment. Accept the truths of these verses: "Never pay back evil for evil. . . . Dear friends, never avenge yourselves. Leave that to God, for he has said that he will repay those who deserve it. [Don't take the law into your own hands.]" (Rom. 12:17, 19 TLB). This forms the basis for principle two:

• Principle 2 •
Don't lash back.

Whenever our pride has been trampled, in addition to knowing the truth that vengeance belongs to the Lord, we need something strong to restrain us from striking back. With the anger stirred up within us, where do we get the strength to hold ourselves in check?

If we daily live in fellowship with Jesus, when our interest or our person is violated or under attack we can at that moment yield up our rights to the Holy

Spirit. As we do, there will come the inner control and love to be a beautiful responder instead of an ugly reactor. We, the children of God, can receive power through the Holy Spirit, if we yield ourselves to His control.

We see this so beautifully illustrated in the martyrdom of Stephen, recorded in the seventh chapter of Acts. We read, "The Jewish leaders were stung to fury by Stephen's accusation, and ground their teeth in rage. . . . Then they mobbed him, putting their hands over their ears, and drowning out his voice with their shouts, and dragged him out of the city to stone him" (Acts 7:54, 57, 58 TLB).

Why did they stone Stephen? All he did was try to lovingly share with them the good news of Jesus Christ. They could have turned him down without killing him. The last thing Stephen deserved was death by stoning. Yet the Acts of the Apostles records these last, forgiving words of Stephen: "And he fell to his knees, shouting, 'Lord, don't charge them with this sin!' and with that, he died" (Acts 7:60 TLB).

How could Stephen keep from reacting with the same kind of rage and violence that he was receiving so unjustly? The Scriptures tell us that Stephen was a man full of the Holy Spirit. To keep from retaliating, like Stephen, we need to yield to the Holy Spirit that part within us that cries out against the unjust treatment. We must trust ourselves to the Spirit of God and believe God will vindicate us when and where we need it.

Make It Work for You. The third principle builds on the first two, perhaps being a composite of them. I want to consider criticism. The first principle ("Accept the reality of unfairness") can further be expanded to mean to accept the fact that you're going to be criticized in life. And the second ("Don't lash back") is especially important for application in the area of what to do when you are criticized. When it comes to handling unjust criticism, put into practice these two guidelines, while moving ahead to:

• **Principle 3** •

Learn from your critics.

A team of sociologists interviewed every resident in a small town in New England. Among other things, they learned that each person admitted to criticizing other men and women in the community.

But each person was enraged to learn that he, in turn, had been criticized by one or more of his neighbors. Think about it. What one of us hasn't at some time been unjustly harsh on another person? Why then should it shock us when we become a target of such attitudes?

Whenever you step out from the crowd, you become a target for unfair criticism. If you're a leader in your family, community, school, church, political circle, or anywhere else, you are going to face this, simply because you have assumed a leadership role. And the bigger your leadership role is, the more attacks you will receive. It comes with the territory. You will note that the greatest leaders in the American church scene are the ones constantly being ridiculed and condemned, not only by the media but by other, less successful people.

Even the motives of Jesus were misunderstood and viciously assaulted. It makes fascinating reading, as you move through the accounts of Jesus' life, to make a list of all the unfair criticism directed against the Son of God. They condemned Jesus for doing good on the Sabbath. They called Him a glutton. They despised Him for being a friend with sinners. They disparaged Him for breaking with tradition. Worst of all, they called Him a Samaritan (John 8:48). This was the lowest, dirtiest description they could imagine. Jesus, the Perfect One, did not live without severe criticism. He did not deserve any of this.

Question: If Jesus faced such attack, who do you think you are that you should live without it? The truth is, you and I are not perfect. No person alive can please all the other imperfect people.

There are only two ways to handle criticism: the wrong way and the right way.

Here is an example of a wrong way to handle criticism. When Lawrence married Louise, she was trim, slim, and a very attractive young woman. Twenty-one years later she had become very flabby. The truth was that he loved her more deeply with the passing years but did not find her flab physically attractive. He also observed that his wife was frequently sick, and he suspected that the root of her problem was her gross overweight. Out of his concern for his wife and for their marriage, he tried in a very gentle, tactful way to get her to face the truth that she desperately needed to trim down. Even though he was not overweight, he offered to go on a diet with her if it would help.

Instead of receiving the truth as it had been communicated in love, Louise became very hostile. Every time he tried to bring up the subject, it ended up with her crying and blaming him for not accepting her as she was.

You know it is hard to face the truth about yourself even when someone who loves you communicates it. But if we can receive the truth and apply it to our lives, what tremendous advancement and growth can take place.

Here is an example of the right way to receive criticism, even when it is unjust. One morning, an executive who had returned from a business trip walked up to his secretary's desk and in front of the whole office staff shouted, "Mary, I told you to put that list of clients' telephone numbers in my briefcase. When I got to Los Angeles and I needed it, it wasn't there. I tried to call you at home, but I couldn't get you. This really messed up my trip, and it's all your fault."

Mary felt embarrassed and humiliated. She knew that she had placed the telephone numbers in her boss's briefcase as instructed. Controlling the anger she felt inside she said, "I'm sorry, Mr. Jones."

Later as Mary sat at her desk she felt she had been mistreated by her boss. She was especially hurt by the way he had humiliated her in front of the other staff members. But instead of sitting there, sulking over her own wounded pride, she intentionally changed her thinking toward her boss. He had been under many stresses and strains lately. His wife had left him. His teenage daughter was on drugs. The firm had lost some of its biggest accounts. She thought, *It's no wonder he is so easily upset.*

About this time one of her friends in the office came to her desk and said, "The old buzzard sure did mistreat you this morning."

Mary smiled and said, "Oh, that's okay. I think the boss is under a lot of stress and strain. I think I'll stay late tonight and see if I can help him get caught up on some of his work." This she did. A few days later the boss sheepishly admitted he had found the missing papers in his briefcase, where they had been all the time. They had a good laugh together, and the incident was forgotten.

Let's admit it. Any criticism is hard to take, and the unjust kind hits us even harder. When someone says we are wrong, we feel threatened and often unloved. Sometimes a boss, parents, teachers, husband or wife, or friends will try to show us our flaws. The big question is: How will we handle that? Why not let your critics help make you successful? They cannot make you a worse person, unless you let them.

Even censure holds potential for your own self-improvement, so listen to it. Have the courage to hear what the person says. Then ask yourself these tough questions. "Is there any grain of truth in it? Is there any lesson here that God has for me?"

You may find that your critics are wrong, completely off base. On the other hand, there may be at least a grain of truth in what they say. Even the most unfriendly and unfair person may see a bit of truth, which, if received and applied to your life, will result in your own betterment.

As children of God, our security rests not in what other people say, but in the fact that God the Father loves us just as we are. Because God loves me, I can be free to accept truths that I need to hear and, with Christ's help, make application of them in my life. I am accepted, and with Christ's help I am becoming.

Winning the Fight. The successful handling of unjust treatment when it comes in your life depends upon the battle within yourself. Within each of us, when we are unjustly treated, a battle rages over whether or not we will surrender leadership to our negative feelings. This bring us to the fourth principle in learning the art of turning the other cheek and getting on top of mistreatment in our lives.

• Principle 4 •

Never surrender leadership to negative feelings.

We all have feelings, and when we are mistreated we know it. We are wounded. Boy, does it hurt to be abused.

When this happens, we must guard against allowing hurt feelings to become ill feelings. You see, in time, hurt feelings will heal up, if we keep the infection of bitterness out. The Bible admonishes us not to let any root of bitterness springing up trouble us and thereby defile many (see Heb. 12:15). As a pastor I see so many people who are wiped out in their relationships because they have allowed a root of bitterness to infect them, from the inside out, in their attitudes and the way they relate to other people. A bitter spirit not only hurts our relationship with the wrongdoer but affects us negatively in all other relationships. You cannot tolerate bitterness within you.

Two different people, about the same age, went through unwanted and undeserved divorces. I don't think anything hurts more than a mate's rejection. Each of these persons' spouses ran off with another lover.

Four years later, one is better and has rebuilt his life. The other, after four years, remains bitter, and her life is still in pieces. What is the difference? The same thing happened to both people. They were cruelly wronged by a trusted mate. But now one is better, while the other one is bitter. The difference? The recovered one refused to surrender leadership of his life to ill feelings, while the other let bitterness take control.

What do you do if your hurt spirit has become infected with bitterness? You confess it to Jesus as sin. You ask Him to come and forgive you and to cleanse you. Even as you ask, He makes you completely clean. Right now, let Him heal you from the ill spirit that's been eating you up.

When our youngest, Scott, was six years of age, he began to learn some tough realities about unjust treatment. While up in the common area of woods three blocks from our home, he was playing with neighborhood boys ranging in age from six to nine. He evidently did something that made one of the older boys angry, for the boy picked up a rock and threw it at Scott, hitting him on the side of the nose and just missing his eye.

The first thing we knew about it was when Scott came running home, bleeding and hurt and crying. Worse than the physical injury was the wounding of his person. Dad and Mom gave him some much needed tender loving care.

We were proud when a couple days later, on his own initiative, our son decided to go back up and face the boy who had injured him. Refusing to surrender to negative emotions, Scott went up to make peace. That day he came home with the relationship mended and renewed.

Moving Forward. Turning the other cheek means something more than just having the right attitude and spirit inside. It means more than accepting the reality of unjust treatment and having enough of Christ's presence and power inside not to lash back. It also means practicing principle five:

• **Principle 5** •

Take positive action.

In the context of the passage in which Jesus tells us to turn the other cheek when unjustly treated, He spells out various positive actions we can take. The twelfth chapter of Romans also spells out such actions. Take note of all of these phrases that illustrate our principle:

"Go the extra mile."

"Love your enemies."

"Pray for those who persecute you."

"Feed your enemy if he's hungry."

"Overcome evil by doing good."

When I have an ill feeling developing toward another as a result of feeling he mistreated me, the quicker I take positive action, the better. The better for me and the better possibility that the relationship will recover and continue.

I have conditioned myself to start praying for the other person. To do so immediately neutralizes my resentment. Then I take the next step and try to do something positive toward the person who has mistreated me. Taking positive action gets me up on top, living and relating out of love instead of buried in the negative.

The only safe and sure way to wipe out an enemy is to make him a friend. How do you do that? By overcoming evil in the power and strength of Jesus Christ, taking positive action, and doing good toward that person who has wronged you.

Recently I read again about Abraham Lincoln's life. To many people Lincoln was many things. To the North he was the preserver of the Union; to the slave, he was a liberator; and to the South he was "the compassionate victor."

On April 10, 1865, four days prior to his death, Abraham Lincoln made this speech to a great crowd gathered to celebrate Lee's surrender. "I see you have a band. I propose now closing up by requesting you to play a certain tune. I've always thought 'Dixie' was one of the best tunes I've ever heard . . . I ask the band to give it a good turn upon it." Lincoln, acting in the spirit of Christ, was making friends out of enemies.

You, too, can master the art of turning the other cheek. You can take positive action that results in making friends out of enemies. Admittedly, not everyone who mistreats you becomes a friend or stays a friend. It does take two people to have a relationship. But no matter how the relationship turns out, you will have the joy of knowing that you have done your part in getting along with difficult people and handling abusive treatment.

IN A CAPSULE

• Principle 1 •
Accept the reality of unfairness.

• Principle 2 •
Don't lash back.

• Principle 3 •
Learn from your critics.

• Principle 4 •
Never surrender leadership to negative feelings.

• Principle 5 •
Take positive action.

 PART III

Getting Along with Those Who Are the Closest

7

Make Friends and Keep Them

Seven principles for having and keeping close friends

L ars Wilhelmsson, in his book *Making Forever Friends*, says, "Friends are a must! We must have friends and be friends to be fully human and alive."

Part of God's design and purpose in creating us was that we might relate in different friendship relationships. That's why trying to live without friends is like trying to eat Cheerios every morning without milk and sweetener. The process goes on, but it is void of all pleasure and fulfillment.

Dr. James J. Lynch, a specialist in psychosomatic diseases, says in his book *The Broken Heart* that loneliness is the number-one cause of illness and death in America today. This renowned doctor vividly contrasts the harmful effects of isolation with the healing power of human contact. Lonely people not only live unhappier lives, but they die sooner than those who enjoy warm relationships.

What cures loneliness? Doing what I'm going to talk about in this chapter: making friends and keeping them. Someone has said: "Friends make a rainy day sunny." Friendship serves not only as medicine to bring healing into your life, but as a preventative.

No other statement in the entire world is more true than this one: *We really do need each other!* Think about these words from the wisdom of Scripture: "Two are better than one. . . . For if they fall, the one will lift up his fellow: but woe to him that is alone when he falleth; for he hath not another to help him up" (Eccles. 4:9, 10).

Three Circles of Friendship

Jesus placed high value on friendship. Even though He came to earth primarily to "seek and save the lost," He still made it a priority in His life to choose and cultivate friends.

Wherever the Lord went, He was keenly interested in the people He met. In His beautiful openness and acceptance, Jesus never excluded anyone, but always reached out to include a new friend.

Wherever Jesus taught, multitudes of pupils gathered around Him. The Gospel accounts also teach us that Jesus chose twelve disciples, who left everything to follow Him and live with Him for the three and one-half years of His public ministry. Have you ever stopped to wonder who were Jesus' close friends?

A study of Jesus' life reveals that He had an outer circle of multitudes of casual friends, a middle circle of the twelve disciples, with whom He spent a lot of time, and an inner circle of a few special friends with whom He shared on the deepest of levels.

Jesus stands as our perfect example of a healthy personality pattern. He was acquainted with multitudes; He was closer to some; and He was very close to a few such as Peter, James, John, Mary, Martha, and Lazarus. The Scriptures say, "Now Jesus loved Martha, and her sister, and Lazarus" (John 11:5). How Jesus loved to go to the home of these three closest friends! It was His home. Here, away from everything else, He would relax, laugh, and enjoy all the benefits of close friendship.

Just as it was in Jesus' life, each of us, to have a healthy personality, needs to learn to get along well in each of these three circles of friendship—inner circle, middle circle, and outer circle.

Up to this point, we have dealt mostly with relationships on the outer circle and the middle circle. Now we turn our full attention to the inner circle.

One giant problem today is that many people don't feel really close to anyone. In the middle and outer circles, we get along with a lot of friends. We have "friends" at church, at work, and in the community— meaning that they do not throw rocks at us; they do not put nails under our tires; they say hello to us; and they give us a few strokes along the way. Still we have a deep, unfulfilled longing to know someone more fully and completely. It is as if our inner being cries out to know and be known. This is called the need for intimacy.

In our mobile and hurried society, it is all too easy to pay attention to everything else and to grossly neglect the cultivation and nurture of the relationships closest to us. When it comes to sharing deeply and relating intimately, even though that is something we all really want, most of us have a lot of room for improvement and growth.

Close Friends Are Priceless

Someone has said: "One close friend is worth more than a thousand acquaintances." When I started out in the ministry, I made a common mistake. I tried to relate well to many people, but did not take the time to smell the roses and cultivate relationships within the inner circle. As I look back now, I can see that, because of this, my life lacked depth, warmth, and fulfillment. This all changed for the better when I learned that taking time to get close to a few people is more important than being able to mail out and receive 1,000 Christmas cards.

A very interesting verse of Scripture says, "A man of many companions may come to ruin" (Prov. 18:24 NIV). What in the world does this mean? Is it bad to have many friends? No, there's nothing wrong with that. This points out the shallowness and emptiness that can overtake us if we spend all our time with an outer circle and middle circle of friends, to the exclusion of developing special friends in the inner circle.

Paul Tournier describes it, "No one can develop freely in this world and find a full life without feeling understood by at least one person." When you have one friend with whom you can share everything and feel accepted and edified, you have a priceless asset in your life. There is no substitute for a close friend.

Seven Principles for Having and Keeping Close Friends

• Principle 1 •

Treat your close friends as you want to be treated.

If you were another person, would you like to have yourself as a close friend? It's a thought to ponder. As we begin this crucial, last section, we come right back to the recurring heartbeat of this book: The key principle for getting along with other people, in whatever circle they are, is to relate to them according to this Golden Rule: "Treat others as you want to be treated."

Emerson told us, "The only way to have a friend is to be a friend." Let me add, "The only way to have a close friend is to be a close friend." And you cannot remain close by neglecting, taking for granted, taking liberties with, or taking advantage of your close friends.

To cultivate and continue close relationships takes not less work, but more work. The things we begin doing that work well for us are the things we must keep on doing.

Dale Carnegie, in his timeless bestseller, *How to Win Friends and Influence People*, tells how dogs know more about making friends than some people. Mr. Carnegie points out that when you get within ten feet of a friendly dog he will begin to wag his tail. If you stop to pet him, he will almost jump out of his skin to show you how much he likes you. A dog makes friends by being genuinely interested in people, not by trying to get people interested in him. Carnegie says, "You can make more friends in two months by becoming interested in other people than you can in two years by trying to get other people interested in you."

To have close friends you must be not a little interested in them, but more interested in them than others. And to keep a close friend you must keep putting forth the effort to be interested in what's going on in his life. Treat a close friend as you want to be treated and keep on treating that close friend as you want to be treated. Paying attention to this foundational principle will take you a long way toward success in getting along with those who are closest to you.

• Principle 2 •

Build your friend's self-esteem.

Lord Chesterfield, in his famous letters to his son, said something like this: "My son, here is the way to get people to like you. Make every person like himself a little better, and I promise that he or she will like you very much."

This principle of building the other person's self-esteem is not less important when it comes to close friendships, but even more important. The people we will feel closest to are those who have discovered how to make us feel good about ourselves as persons. Oliver Wendell Holmes said, "Friendship is a pleasing game of interchanging praise."

When I was a teenager, growing up back in Columbus, Ohio, each summer I worked on the church campgrounds, directly across from our house. During summer camp I spent a lot of time talking and conversing with a pastor named Joseph Nielson.

Although Joe was ten to fifteen years older than me, he always talked to me as if I were an equal. He made me feel so good about myself. He listened to all my questions, my doubts, my searchings, and accepted me where I was. At the same time he conveyed to me that he believed in me and that God was going to use my life in some great way.

Because of the thousands of miles that separate us now, I sometimes go for years without seeing this close friend. Whenever I think of him, however, I experience warm and good feelings. And when we do meet after long times of separation, immediately we have a great conversation to share.

Building a friend's self-esteem means committing yourself to helping that friend be successful in his achievements. Too many people mar their close friendships with petty jealousies. We read, "When others are happy, be happy with them. If they are sad, share their sorrow" (Rom. 12:15 TLB). Make a commitment to your close friends to do everything in your power to help them fulfill the desires of their hearts. Then, when they succeed, you will succeed with them. Help others fulfill their dreams, and your dreams for friendship will not go unfulfilled.

• Principle 3 •

Pay attention to the little things.

Isn't it interesting that the closer a relationship is supposed to be, the easier it is to become careless about the little things? We have to guard constantly that we do not forget to pay attention to the little things. Those little, extra acts of kindness bind special friends together in the first place. We must not lose that sensitivity and responsiveness.

A dear friend whom I have known for more than a decade phoned me the other day just to say, "I wanted to let you know, Dale, that I appreciate you and am praying for your continuing success in the ministry." When I hung up the phone, I bowed my head and thanked God for that special person and his encouragement. Only a few weeks later I had an opportunity to express some thoughts of kindness back to him.

The little things like a kindness, courtesy, and thoughtfulness mean so much that we can't afford to neglect them. If we do, the friendship begins to die. Remember the little things and keep your close friendships breathing with life and vitality. As an old nursery rhyme put it:

> It's the little things we do or say
> That make or break the beauty of the
>   average passing day.
> Hearts, like doors, will open with ease
> To very, very little keys,
> And don't forget that two of these
> Are "I thank you," and "If you please."

• Principle 4 •

Take off the mask, and let your
friends get close to you.

In chapter one, we said that people are drawn to the person who opens up and shares his true self. Now we want to take this a step further and see that you cannot feel inner-circle intimate with another person until you take the mask off and share yourself.

People can know you only as you allow them to know you. Those who never dare to take their masks off and share themselves as they really are can never know the joys of close friendship. Enriched is the person who has learned the wisdom of this old Swedish proverb. "Shared joy is doubled. Shared sorrow is half a sorrow." The heart of friendship is in sharing yourself openly with another person.

We all hide and keep secrets from three classes of people:

- Those who are enemies and might use our secrets against us.
- Those we think unworthy of our self-revelations.
- Those we do not know well enough to take our masks off and disclose ourselves.

There remains this enormous need to share deeply with someone—or two or three. I need someone with whom I can safely open my heart.

Jesus had that need in His own life. That's why He took James, John, and Peter aside from all the others and opened up His heart to them. He thought them ready to hear things that others should not. He needed to share deeply with His closest friends. And in order for them to know Him, His motives, and His feelings as He faced death at the cross, they had to listen. If Jesus required this in His life, how much more you and I need it.

If a close friend is truly a friend, he or she will love you all the more for having shared yourself deeply. You can place no greater confidence in another person than to let him or her know you on the deeper levels. The people who we allow to know us this way are those with whom we are going to feel the closest bond.

• **Principle 5** •

Be a giver, not a taker.

I know a woman who desires companionship so deeply that she relates to others almost out of desperation. But she is so busy trying to make friends, trying to have people relate to her the way she wants them to, that she forgets that she must give before she can get. Close friendship requires deep commitment. Giving time and energy required to foster deep relationships is costly and demanding.

Most of the problems people have with their inner circle stem from the lack of giving first. For example, show me a marriage that is falling apart, and I'll show you two people who are trying to get from each other, instead of giving first.

Learning to give first helped in the Brown home. "Our marriage wasn't exactly on the rocks," Dennis said. "It was more like a cold war. The warmth and affection had gone out of our relationship."

Dennis and his wife, Kathy, were like two strangers living in the same home, not smiling, not touching, hardly ever talking to each other. Dennis says, "I wanted Kathy to show me affection first."

Kathy says, "I wanted Dennis to first give to me, then I would give back to him." So it went on.

Then one Sunday, the Browns came and listened to my sermon. In God's perfect timing, that summer day I was talking about how to have a happy home. During the sermon I said, "I know there are people here today who have fallen out of love, who at one time were much in love. But I tell you today that if you will give first, I believe you can fall back in love."

Unknown to me at the time, God took those words and used them to speak to the Browns. Later reporting what happened, Dennis said, "That morning, you asked everyone to join hands with the person accompanying him or her and to pray with you. We squirmed uncomfortably. Kathy sort of glanced at me, and I glanced back. Actually, we felt embarrassed. But we decided to put our feelings aside and try it.

"From that morning, when we started praying together, our whole relationship began to change. It was in a small way at first. When I'd come home in the evenings, Kathy would have the house shining and be in the kitchen, humming softly as she prepared the evening meal. She would greet me with a smile and a kiss, and I found myself giving in return, being more thoughtful, helping with the children and the house. Then one day we realized that we were in love again. The change started when we let God teach us to give first."

• Principle 6 •

Give your friends the priceless gift
of nonjudgmental acceptance.

A few weeks ago one of our New Hope family handed me a sheet of paper with these words: "A friend is one who knows you as you are, understands where you've been, accepts who you have become, and still gently invites you to grow. Jesus is my best friend."

What a friend we have in Jesus. He loves us regardless of where we have been. He accepts us where we are and as we are. First He gives us His friendship and then He invites us to grow.

In John 13 we read the vivid story of Jesus washing the disciples' feet at the Last Supper. I find it absolutely astonishing that Jesus, knowing full well what Judas would do, went ahead and washed Judas's feet, just as He did His other friends'. Knowing Judas was going to betray Him, He still accepted and loved the man and allowed him the right to make his own wrong decision.

Close friendship does not mean ownership. So often, as people become closer, they take that as the green light to start trying to change each other into the person each wants the other to be. At best this causes tension instead of relaxation, and at worst it rips the relationship apart and destroys it.

Why do we think we have to change those closest to us? We need to remind ourselves of the Bible's words, "Love is not possessive" (1 Cor. 13:5 AP). Love does not smother the life out of a friendship. Giving ourselves the benefit of the doubt, we could say that we try to change the person close to us because we want what's best for him or her. This is kidding ourselves. If we want what's best, we will back off, give him or her our nonjudgmental acceptance, and allow that person the freedom to make mistakes.

One Sunday preceding Thanksgiving, I challenged the people who sat under my ministry to write a letter expressing their thanks to someone. I was delighted to receive this letter from a close friend: "I admire and respect you very much—not because I imagine you are perfect, but because I know you're not but deal so well with the tests and failures that accompany all of us in our humanity."

• Principle 7 •

Stick by your friends through thick and thin.

Someone has said, "A friend is one who walks in when the whole world walks out." Another wise saying is this: "A good friend is like toothpaste. He comes through in a tight squeeze." If you want your friendships to last, then stick with your friends through thick and thin and be loyal. Loyalty is a key to enjoying lasting friendships. What a beautiful, close relationship David and Jonathan had. The Bible describes it with the words "knit together," or, "one in spirit" (see 1 Sam. 18:1).

As David began to rise to the top, like cream, and was placed in authority over Jonathan, instead of becoming jealous, Jonathan felt elated over his advancement. Later when Jonathan's father, King Saul, became envious of David and sought to destroy him, Jonathan stood by his friend. Saul sought to kill David, and Jonathan went to David and expressed his concern and loyalty with these words: "Whatsoever thy soul desireth, I will even do it for thee" (1 Sam. 20:4). Jonathan even risked his own life to stand by and save David. This kind of loyalty makes close friendships pass the test of the storms that come and go.

There is One who will stick with you through anything and everything that you go through in your life. His name is Jesus. You are His close friend—think of it! The world's greatest person, Jesus, wants to be your loyal, lasting Friend. Listen to these glorious words from John 15:15: "But I have called you friends." Whatever you need in the inner circle of your life, your Friend stays with you, helping you, teaching you, and leading you into making that inner circle warmth last.

···················· **IN A CAPSULE** ····················

• Principle 1 •
Treat your close friends as you want to be treated.

• Principle 2 •
Build your friend's self-esteem.

• Principle 3 •
Pay attention to the little things.

• Principle 4 •
*Take off the mask, and let your
friends get close to you.*

• Principle 5 •
Be a giver, not a taker.

• Principle 6 •
*Give your friends the priceless gift
of nonjudgmental acceptance.*

• Principle 7 •
Stick by your friends through thick and thin.

8

Making Marriage a Lasting Affair

Eight ways to avoid adultery

Ed Wheat, in his enriching marriage book entitled *Love Life*, says, "Most people think of a love affair as a passionate interlude between a man and a woman who are not married—at least not to each other. The world, for centuries, has tried to convince people of the notion that secretive adulterous love is more exciting than love in marriage. But the dictionary defines love affair as 'affinity between two persons . . . a particular experience of being in love.'"

Admittedly, illicit affairs, from appearances, seem to be exciting for a little while, but the end result is always devastating and destructive both to the persons involved and their families and friends. I've seen a lot of pain in human beings, but the most excruciating hurt in people's eyes comes from illicit affairs.

Satan's favorite tactic is to give us the counterfeit, make it look like the real thing, and in the end we reap the heartbreak and destruction. First he baits us, then he hooks us, and finally we have been had.

For every counterfeit there exists a real thing. And when it comes to having a lasting love affair, the real thing is what God has designed for husband and wife to enjoy through a lifetime of marriage. In Ecclesiastes 9:9 (TLB) we read these exciting words: "Live happily with the woman you love through the fleeting days of life, for the wife God gives you is your best reward down here for all your earthly toil."

The marriage affair has the potential of being the zenith in friendship. No other relationship gives as many opportunities for such intimacy. We all long for this closeness, this depth sharing, this feeling of at-oneness. When a married couple has achieved this, it is ecstasy. No other relationship can climb to the summit like this one.

If, in your marriage, you're not enjoying this warmth, the answer is not to break your vows by seeking fulfillment through adultery. That bad choice only leads to more isolation, separation, pain, and destruction. Instead dig in and work to bring about that feeling of oneness that your heart so desires. I offer you these tools:

Eight Words and Principles to Make Your Marriage Intimate and Lasting

Word 1: Commitment. A young man just graduated from college said to me, "I'm not going to get married, ever!" A few days later I overheard a divorced lady say, "There is no way that I'm ever going to get married again." These two people had one thing in common. They both had a distorted and cynical view of the relationship.

It's time that someone stands up and speaks this truth: "There's nothing wrong with marriage. It is people that have the problem." It's not *less* commitment that's needed, but *more* commitment.

Most of us are familiar with these words from the marriage vow, "For better for worse, for richer for poorer, in sickness and in health, to love and to cherish, till death us do part." The first ingredient in the making of a close marriage is described in these words of commitment, found in Genesis 2:24: "Therefore shall a man leave his father and his mother, and shall cleave unto his wife: and they shall be one flesh." The first principle for making your marriage a lasting affair is:

* **Principle 1** *

Leave and cleave.

To "leave and cleave" means to commit yourself to the marriage as the primary relationship of your life. When you do this, every other relationship becomes secondary—job, children, education, sports, and everything else. In your priorities, everything else must become secondary to your commitment to make your marriage work and last.

Too many people marry with little or no understanding of the words they say. Before long their vows are tested, for people can't live together very long without seeing each other's raw faults. Mr. Terrific or Mrs. Wonderful suddenly becomes the monster or the witch. When reality hits, disillusionment sets in.

At this point, if the marriage is to become an intimate and lasting affair, the two people must make the commitment to accept and love each other as is, faults and all. Nowhere else is this Bible verse more appropriate: "Love makes up for many of your faults" (Eph. 5:2 TLB).

While "leave and cleave" means the marriage takes first place over other family ties, it does not mean in-laws should be rejected. Establishing some bylaws on in-laws can help. They should include:

- Being loyal, first of all to your mate.
- Not making negative remarks about your mate to any of your relatives.
- Not listening to any negative comments from your relatives about your mate.

- Honoring and respecting your mate's relatives, simply because you love your mate.

Making marriage the primary relationship is important not only for newlyweds, but for all married people. Women often mistakenly put their children above their husband. Sometimes a woman will go back to school or into the workforce, which by itself is fine, except when she puts that above the marriage relationship. Men, in their drive for success, often neglect their wives and families. The jock obsessed with sports may make his wife and kids secondary. Whenever a man or woman, for whatever reason, puts anything or anyone ahead of the spouse, it's opening the lid of Pandora's box.

In recent years of ministry, I've come to see how crucial the principle "to leave and cleave" is to the success of a remarriage in the mixing of two families. Those personally involved in the complex blending of two families into one know that *The Brady Bunch* hardly tells the whole story of a your-kids-my-kids household. Regluing the shreds from former fractures into a new composite is often both painstaking and painful.

When children from a former marriage are brought into a new marriage, the adjustments multiply. An almost overwhelming complexity of relationships exists. Children affected by the pressure of divided loyalties often work to sabotage a new marriage.

Then there is always that continuing battle over "you don't love my kids like I do." Truly the new mate will probably never have the same emotional attachment to your children that you have. How do you respond to all the complexity and raw emotions one encounters in trying to bring together two families into one?

The answer is in principle one, taken from Genesis 2:24: "leave and cleave." In its context, "leave and cleave" refers to leaving father and mother, but the principle applies to leaving *anything* that could come between you as husband and wife. This means that whatever has happened in the past, you've got to let go of it and leave it in the past. And it means that whatever confusion might be going on in the present, you've got to back off from it and get your priorities straight. You need to reaffirm your number-one priority: commitment to your marriage as the primary relationship in your life. When you get this right, so many other things fall into place. Wise people keep focused on working hard to make their marriage close and lasting.

Whether this is your first one or a remarriage, you've got to get away together from all the pressures and problems of life. You need times to be communicative, to be friends and lovers. In a second marriage these are not less important; they are essential to your relationship's life and well-being. Sometimes it takes hours and more hours to talk through the complexities of emotions and problems, to come to a mutually satisfying solution. This takes a lot of commitment.

Word 2: Companionship. A woman went to an attorney to seek a divorce. "So," said the attorney, "you want a divorce on the grounds that your husband is careless about his appearance."

"That's right," said the woman, "he hasn't made an appearance in over three years."

Living apart, or living together but doing everything separately, is not the way to enjoy closeness in a marriage. God created us with a need for companionship. How can you fulfill this need? By practicing this principle:

• Principle 2 •
Become best friends.

Do this by spending time together. If you have demanding schedules, then plan and make the time to be together, work together, play together, and most of all, enjoy conversation together. Cause your lives to become intertwined. Be easy to talk to. This may mean that you have to be a little laid back. Don't be too quick to jump in with both feet and give your opinion or judgment, but simply listen with interest and love. Allow your mate the freedom to express ideas and feelings without your having to straighten him or her out. If you can do this, you will keep growing closer together, and you will be best friends. I'm so proud to tell people that my wife, Margi, is my best friend. And she feels that way about me.

Recently in our Portland paper was a story about a couple named Theodore and Lydia, who died together in their home. When found, they were on the floor, in each other's arms.

As the story goes, apparently the woman, who was eighty-seven, had a heart attack while sitting on the sofa. Her husband, eighty-nine, went to the telephone to call for help. Then Lydia apparently fell from the sofa onto the floor, and her husband immediately went to her, lay down beside her, and took her in his arms. He must have been very agitated, and he died with her. Even in death they were inseparable.

Word 3: Comradeship. I heard a story about a man who had been married for more than forty-five years. Returning home one afternoon, he found his wife packing. "What are you doing?" he asked.

"I can't stand it here anymore!" she cried. "All the years of fighting, arguing, bickering—I'm leaving!"

The gentleman stood there for a moment, bewildered, watching her struggle through the door with her packed suitcases. Suddenly he ran into the bedroom and snatched a suitcase from the shelf. Dashing out to the porch, he yelled, "Wait a minute! I can't stand it anymore either. I'm going with you."

This little story introduces the subject of comradeship, but hardly does it justice. A beautiful true story illustrates it better. A couple celebrating their twenty-fifth wedding anniversary were asked the secret of their close relationship. The wife replied for them both, saying, "We decided right from the start that it was us against the world—two people forming a majority of one. So whatever happened, or however much we clashed in private, we stuck by each other. We were like a brother and sister on the playground. We might scrap with each other, but let an outsider try to attack one of us, and he had to take us both on. If one of us hurt, the other wiped away the tears. If one had a project to achieve, then the other pitched in, and together we achieved it."

Comradeship is spelled out in this very important phrase from the Bible, "They shall be one flesh" (Gen. 2:24). From this comes the corresponding principle:

• Principle 3 •

Practice oneness.

What a beautiful thing happens in a marriage relationship when two people get on the same team! It is amazing what two people can achieve when they work at it together. Practicing oneness means that you are not competing but completing. Not alone, but together.

Before any person can have closeness in marriage, he or she must stop acting like a spoiled superstar and become a member of the team. You see, it's not "my money," it's "our money." It's not "your problem," but it's "our problem." It's not what "I want," but it's "what's best for our marriage together."

You may further experience this feeling if you make it a practice to give your mate your loyal support. It gives me great inner strength to know that whatever I'm facing on the job or in any other part of my life, Margi is always for me and never against me. Now that doesn't mean she doesn't give me a piece of her mind from time to time in private. But it means we're on a team and we help each other be successful. There isn't anything that I wouldn't do to help my wife to use all her potential and fulfill her dreams. We have made the wonderful discovery that we are so much more together than either of us is alone. What strength, what growth, and what joy come from being comrades.

Word 4: Communication. I asked a friend who had been married successfully for more than half a century about the secret of his and his wife's closeness. He said, "Oh, we've had our problems like everyone else, but we've always been able to sit down and talk them out." Then he added, "Any two people who live together are going to have some misunderstandings. But I've never seen a problem yet but what could be worked out if two people would keep on conversing openly and freely in a spirit of love."

It's my observation that estrangement creeps into a marriage not so much from what is said as from what goes unsaid. As a pastor, I don't worry so much about the married people in my congregation who experience a little difference of opinion. But I become very concerned about those who stop communicating with each other. This next principle is the life and health of the marriage relationship.

• Principle 4 •

To reveal is better than to conceal.

Whatever happens, never stop expressing yourself—just learn to do it better. Prolonged silence is not golden; it is a cruel weapon. Phyllis McGinley penned these words: "Words can sting like anything, but silence breaks the heart." When the flow of communication stops, things deteriorate quickly. I've known of husbands and wives who go for days without speaking to each other. At the breakfast table the father says, "Johnny, tell your mother to pass the bacon." This is pure destruction. It allows stubbornness and anger to rule instead of giving the person closest to you the Golden Rule treatment.

In this crucial area the Bible gives us some tremendous instruction when it says, "Let not the sun go down upon your wrath" (Eph. 4:26). In a marriage relationship, when there's a misunderstanding, we should run eagerly to get it straightened out.

Feel close to each other by keeping the barriers down and the communication flowing. Communication is like a mountain stream. As it flows it makes everything so crystal clear.

Word 5: Compromise. Some people mistakenly view compromise as a sign of weakness. But if it is a weakness, then, tell me, why is it so difficult for people to do?

It takes an enormous amount of strength and character to achieve this. In practicing this type of concession you cannot lie down and let the marriage partner walk over you and do anything he or she wants. Rather understand and practice this:

• Principle 5 •

Two heads are better than one.

Two people see twice as much as one person. No one has all the facts or all the answers. What an asset to have two viewpoints! The Bible teaches us that there is great strength in getting different vantage points. We all have our limitations and our blind spots. It's not a matter of who's right or who's wrong, but what's best for us together.

There's a big difference between *accommodation* and *compromise*. Accommodation means agreeing with the other person and acting as if everything is okay, when it isn't. To accommodate without having expressed yourself denies the validity of your own feelings and the worth of your own opinion and ideas. When you do this, you end up angry at yourself and feeling a low sense of self-esteem. Neither do you have good feelings toward the person you've accommodated.

A while back I counseled with a beautiful Christian couple. I could hardly believe they were on the verge of divorce. From outward appearance, their eight years of marriage seemed good. They didn't fight or yell at each other. There was no abuse or unfaithfulness. Outwardly, they were cordial, even kind and considerate of each other. What then had created the gulf between them? As we talked it surfaced that both of them had made it a habit to be accommodating, without ever expressing their own true feelings.

The young man, brought up in a home with an overbearing, verbally abusive father, made up his mind that the last thing in the world he wanted to do was to be like his father. So when he married, instead of expressing any feelings that would disagree with his wife's wants or demands, he suppressed them and made it a habit to accommodate her.

All the time he thought he was being so nice, he was storing up unresolved anger. After years of denying his true emotions, as he sat in my office he said, "I do not love her." All the time he hated himself for not living up to the biblical standard, "Husbands, love your wives" (Eph. 5:25).

As we shared together I explained the difference between accommodating and compromise. I pointed out that in a good marriage there has got to be a lot of compromise. This occurs when two people each have been given the opportunity to speak their minds, to fully express their feelings and ideas about the issue at hand. Mutual expression and listening take place. Each puts himself in the other person's shoes to see it from the other's viewpoint. Finally the give-and-take through dialogue results in a shared decision.

Word 6: Compassion. If you feel you must hide your hurts from your partner, something is wrong in either you or the other person that needs to be corrected. In this troubled world we all need an emotional refuge. God intended the marriage relationship to provide that kind of sensitive, caring, compassionate relationship. Two people in a marriage draw close when they become each other's shoulder to cry on.

Some of the closest moments that my wife and I have shared have been in each other's arms, taking turns to comfort the beloved one. To really get close to your mate:

* **Principle 6** *

Go beyond sympathy, with empathy.

Many years ago I heard this unforgettable story: A young mother left her small child unattended while she was doing laundry in the basement. The child found some adult medicine, drank it all, and was dead upon arrival at the hospital.

The mother sat, stunned and stricken, waiting for her husband to come. What would he say? He idolized the child. When he did come, he took his wife in his arms and said just four words, over and over: "Darling, I love you." Nothing else, no questions, no incriminations, no blame. Just, "Darling, I love you."

That man knew how to be a compassionate husband. Forgetting his own hurt and thinking only of his wife, he drew a protective cloak around this suffering woman.

When you learn to go beyond sympathy and enter into your mate's life with tenderness, understanding, and empathy, you're going to feel so close.

Word 7: Celebrate. A middle-aged couple had just gone to sleep when their smoke alarm went off. The husband jumped out of bed, dashed into the hall, and then back into the bedroom. "The whole back end of the house is on fire!" he shouted.

Grabbing his wife by the arm, he led her down the smoke-filled hallway and out the front door. As the husband opened the door to safety, he glanced at his wife and saw a smile on her face. "Good grief!" He inquired, "What have you got to be smiling about now?"

"I can't help it," she replied. "This is the first night we've gone out together in five years!"

A termite eats away at the joy of marriage when a couple no longer makes the time to have fun together. It's all too easy to allow responsibilities and routines to completely take over our lives.

To keep romance alive and to enjoy the flow of positive vibrations, you've got to keep getting out of your rut and having some fun together. You cannot afford to stop courting and dating.

As a marriage counselor, I recommend that every married couple from time to time read the Song of

Solomon together. Why? Because when you get into the spirit of that magnificent romantic book of the Bible, you get a feeling that this principle makes a marriage exciting:

• Principle 7 •
Live joyfully together.

Word 8: Christ. The final principle to make your marriage a joy-filled, lasting affair is:

• Principle 8 •
Put Christ first.

The presence and lordship of Jesus in a marriage relationship blesses it, lifts it, and gives it the constant renewal of fresh love. When Jesus was on earth, He went to the wedding at Cana of Galilee. A problem developed: They ran out of wine for the wedding feast. The couple was getting off on the wrong foot.

Then it happened. Jesus worked a miracle and turned the water into wine. Not just any ordinary wine, but superb stuff. In every marriage at times the wine of joy runs out. The marriage needs a touch, a renewal. It's at these moments that the wise husband and wife fall on their knees together before Jesus, put Him first in their commitments, their love, and their marriage. At that moment, Jesus will bring His miracle of closeness and love to the marriage relationship.

When two hearts open completely to Jesus, there comes healing, forgiveness, and overflowing love. Together in Christ we become one, immovable and inseparable.

These eight words and their corresponding principles will help you feel closer to your mate and make your marriage a lasting affair. All this truth and understanding could be summed up in a paraphrase of our Golden Rule principle: "Treat your mate as you want to be treated."

························· **IN A CAPSULE** ·························

• Principle 1 •
Leave and cleave.

• Principle 2 •
Become best friends.

• Principle 3 •
Practice oneness.

• Principle 4 •
To reveal is better than to conceal.

• Principle 5 •
Two heads are better than one.

• Principle 6 •
Get beyond sympathy, with empathy.

• Principle 7 •
Live joyfully together.

• Principle 8 •
Put Christ first.

9

Are You Easy to Live With?

Eight dos and don'ts for getting along with your everyday people

How easy are you to live with? This could be a threatening question. I've thought about it, even gone so far as to ask my wife about it. First she kind of grinned and didn't answer. So I took the plunge and asked her again, and this time she replied: "Well—maybe there's room for a little improvement." Actually there's probably room for a lot of improvement.

The basic problem in any marriage or family situation is learning how to live in an intimate situation and control your anger. We all rub each other the wrong way in any close contact, and we have to learn how to control anger, irritations, and daily frustrations.

If you really want to get along well with those nearest to you, then courageously ask yourself some honest questions:

1. Am I relaxed with the people closest to me, or am I uptight?
2. Do I treat those I live with or relate to on a daily basis as I want to be treated, or do I mistreat them by taking liberties I would not take with someone I want to impress?
3. Do I seem to be rubbing my children, mate, or special friend the wrong way? What kind of vibrations am I sending out to those closest to me?

Let's be honest. When it comes to being easy to live with, each of us can stand some improvement. I confess that my personal goal is to keep growing in this area.

Four Don'ts to Help You Become Easier to Live With

• Principle 1 •
Don't be touchy.

When I first started out in the pastoral ministry, my touchiness caused my feelings to get hurt a lot. My wise father, who had been a minister for fifty years, gave me some advice. "Son, if you're going to make it in the ministry, you're going to have to get a little more tough skinned." What was he saying? Don't allow yourself to get hurt and despondent over every little thing. In other words, "Don't go around wearing your feelings on your sleeve."

We most need this concept in the inner circle of our lives. Sometimes we expect those closest to us not only to understand intuitively what we're thinking, but to respond sympathetically to it. When they don't, we get our feelings hurt. That's being too touchy. How can that close person know what you're thinking or what your needs are unless you have spoken of them?

We need to be reminded that everyone has pressures and problems. It helps so much when we try to understand what's going on that day in someone's life. A man comes home, and his wife is all upset. Instead of getting his own feelings hurt, he needs to find out what occurred to frazzle and frustrate her. If the man is too touchy about his own feelings, he's going to miss the opportunity to tune in to and express understanding and love for that special woman.

In daily life, people exaggerate and say a lot of things they don't mean. They also make statements that they don't take time to explain. A sharp word spoken or a kind word left unspoken does not mean that your friend, mate, child doesn't love you. Be careful, in relating to everyday life, that you do not make mountains out of molehills. Don't be touchy, and you will be much easier to live with.

• Principle 2 •

Don't be a reactor.

Human nature has not changed over the years. Sometimes we forget that Jesus' disciples were human beings, just like us. Because they lived close together, they had their difficulties.

Luke's Gospel records that Jesus steadfastly set His face toward Jerusalem as He went to fulfill His mission. Along the way, He traveled through a Samaritan village, where He wanted to stay overnight. "But they were turned away! The people of the village refused to have anything to do with them because they were headed for Jerusalem" (Luke 9:53 TLB). There was not only animosity, but open hostility between the Samaritans and the Jews. James and John reacted by wanting to call fire down from heaven and burn them up.

We often respond in much the same way in our close relationships. Our mate, child, or friend bothers us or fails to do something we want done, and the impulse is to retaliate. That's like lighting the fuse on a firecracker: It starts a chain reaction that sets off a bigger explosion.

When we choose to react, we lose control. We create hostility and conflict. Reason is thrown out the door.

Living together requires that we increasingly learn to control our emotions so that we will not be reactors. Most people have certain emotional buttons that, when pushed, go off and cause a predictable backlash. Growth in learning to relate better to those closest to us involves discovering these buttons and reprogramming them. When we hear a certain word or are treated in a particular way, we do not have to let negative responses make donkeys out of us. With God's power, we can change.

Many people have been brought up in homes with a lot of reacting and conflict. They tend to become the perpetrator and inflictor of reactions or go to the other extreme and become the silent accommodator. Neither way is good.

Learn to control yourself by not flying off the handle. When you have something to say, say it in a positive way. Do this, and you will be much easier to live with.

• Principle 3 •
Don't be picky.

Picky people are no fun to live with. I know a man who has the possibilities of being a beautiful husband and a good father, but at every dinner, family members sit around the table in fear of being singled out by Dad. This is so bad that everyone in the family suffers from stomach problems. If the son has mowed the yard, the father complains he didn't do it correctly. Or his wife didn't cook the meat to suit him. Or one of the daughters doesn't have her hair combed right. No matter how hard the family tries to please him, something is wrong. It's pick, pick, pick. This man is difficult, if not impossible, for his family members to live with.

The man's friendships are no different. He has been known to go on a tirade, picking apart his "closest friend." He's a hard man to get along with.

That picking disease can creep into our lives, if we let it. Don't allow it. I want to be positive and uplifting. What kind of words does your tongue speak to those closest to you? Recently I read that the speech center of our brain has control over all our nervous system. In other words, what we say directly affects our nerves. It affects not only our nerves, but others' nerves, too. What we say greatly affects the people we live with. Do you know you can actually make the people you live with physically ill by speaking critical, negative words? On the other hand, when you speak positive, uplifting words you bring health to the bodies of those you love.

A big step in being an easy person to live with and getting along beautifully with people closest to you is to gain control over your own tongue.

• **Principle 4** •

Don't be harsh and judging.

When we are harsh and judgmental of those we relate to in the inner circle, love goes right out the window. With people close to us we at times take liberties we would not take in more distant relationships. For example, we set up in our minds an expectation or standard for others, never asking them if that's something they accept for themselves; then when they don't perform well or come up to our expectations, we become the judge and jury and harshly condemn them. The question we have to ask ourselves is this: Who gave us this?

An interesting insight into the close friendship between the apostles Peter and John comes out of chapter 21 in John's Gospel. This is a post-Resurrection appearance of Jesus to His disciples at the Sea of Tiberias. After the disciples eat dinner as Jesus' guests, He takes Peter aside for some one-on-one dialogue. Jesus three times asks Peter how much he really loves Him. Each time Peter strongly affirms his love.

Jesus tells Peter what his ministry is going to be and also about the hardship that he's going to endure. Peter turns his eyes on John the Beloved and wants to know, "What shall this man do?"

Every time we start getting our eyes fixed on what a close friend or mate should or should not do, we have crossed over the line. We have taken upon ourselves a responsibility that is not ours. At that point, we must remind ourselves of this: "I'm not accountable for anybody else's attitudes and actions, only for my own."

In a classic answer to Peter, Jesus penetrated this kind of wrongdoing by saying, "What is that to thee? Follow thou me" (John 21:22). In other words: It's none of your business, Peter, what your close friend, John, does or doesn't do. You're answerable only for what you do and say.

Get off the judgment seat, get on the mercy seat, and live relaxed.

Four Dos That Make You Easy to Live With

• Principle 1 •
Do talk it out.

We're all tempted to think communication of an unfavorable feeling tends to make waves. If something you do bothers me, I may think it would be better not to mention it, falsely believing that our relationship will be better for it. So I keep it inside myself.

Then some little dinky thing happens, and I explode. All the while you annoyed me, I kept it inside somewhere, secretly learning to hate you. When the explosion came, you didn't understand—and I surprised myself.

It all started when I said, "I don't like what he is doing, but it would be better not to say anything. The relationship will be more peaceful." What I did was not avoid trouble, but save up dynamite for the big explosion.

To be an easier person to live with, practice opening up instead of closing up and building up for the blowup.

• Principle 2 •

Do allow other opinions.

The Sunday school teacher explained freedom of worship to the class. "Why did the Puritans come to this country?" she asked.

"To worship in their own way and make other people do the same," one of the pupils replied.

Isn't it interesting how we want our freedom of speech? I mean, we'll fight for it. But then we turn around and don't want to give the same freedom to the people close to us. We can relieve so much tension and friction in our lives by granting others the right to have their own separate opinions.

Never decide you have to prove yourself right and the person closest to you wrong. You may have a tremendous gift of debate to be able to prove him or her wrong and yourself right, but what have you gained? Is the person going to like you for it? No! Your attitude may cause strain or could even fracture and lead to the breaking of the relationship.

Respect the people you care for most! Give them their dignity, their viewpoint, and in a discussion or disagreement, give them, even if they are wrong, the privilege of saving face. Do this and you will continue to feel close to your loved ones.

We need to learn that Christ wants us to disagree agreeably. Express your opinions, but at the same time, allow the people near you to completely express theirs. Meanwhile, keep the spirit of love as your primary goal in the relationship. If you really practice 1 Corinthians 14:1 (AP), "Make love your number-one aim," you will be a much more relaxed, enjoyable person. In other words, value the other person's viewpoint as much as you value your own. Treat him as you want to be treated.

• Principle 3 •

Do be more tolerant.

The saying "No one is perfect" is so familiar it seems almost trivial. Yet why do the imperfections in those inner-circle people shock us so? Familiarity does reveal it all.

Now at home, if my wife didn't overlook some of my faults, we'd be in big trouble. I thank God that Margi practices the beautiful principle found in Ephesians 4:2 (TLB): "Be humble and gentle. Be patient with each other, making allowance for each other's faults because of your love."

Making allowances for the faults in others comes from an honest confession of your own humanity.

Years ago, in one of my first pastorates, I encountered a woman—I thought she was a friend—who had become disillusioned with me and was leaving our church because of its imperfections. Ours was, I think, her eighth church in as many years. When she walked into my office and made her big announcement, I must have been feeling a little ornery, because I said to her in effect, "I hope you find your perfect church, but I have an idea that if you join it, it won't be perfect any longer." Being that directly truthful was not appropriate. She stormed out the door and never came back.

If such a thing happened today, I would be more tolerant and use a much gentler approach, while trying to help her see that none of us are perfect, not even those of us who live in close fellowship within the church. No relationship can survive without tolerance, and certainly close ones will not thrive and last without a lot of overlooking of one another's faults.

• Principle 4 •

Do stay right with God.

A little girl interrupted her nightly prayer, "Pardon me, God, while I go and kick my brother."

Most of the time I find that when I am disturbed with a member of my inner circle, it shows that something's wrong with my own attitude and spirit. Usually I've not been spending enough time with my heavenly Father. The Scriptures clearly teach us that God is not the author of confusion or disturbance.

When we spend the time with Him to have our minds renewed and our hearts lined up with love, we become His instruments through which peace flows. If we are in contact and fellowship with God, we can even be peaceful when everyone else is storming.

The world's greatest teaching on human relationships was given by Jesus in the Sermon on the Mount. Most of these principles have been directly and indirectly interwoven throughout our journey in getting along. Right in the middle of His teaching, Jesus interjected this foundational truth: "But seek ye first the kingdom of God, and his righteousness; and all these things shall be added unto you" (Matt. 6:33).

The man had been in for counseling four times in two weeks. Each session consisted of his blaming his estranged wife for everything that went wrong. Finally after having listened with compassion, on the fourth time I gently asked, "What about your own actions and behavior? How is your relationship with God?" Then I said, "I've done everything that I can do to help you. There's nothing more that I can do for you until you go and spend the time with God to get your own heart back on track and to get your own attitude straightened out. At this point, anything else is wasting time for both of us."

God used these sincere words to bring this man to the point of surrender. After he left my office he felt angry. Later in the day, however, he realized that he, not his wife or someone else, needed help from the Lord. That man got on his knees and confessed his own sins, the wrong things he'd been doing with other women, and the bitterness he had toward his wife. And the Lord Jesus came and forgave him, cleaned him up, and made him a changed person.

Once this man got right with God, it wasn't long until he was able to get his relationship straightened out with his wife. Let Jesus take over your attitudes and direct your actions, and you will become an easier person to live with. How beautiful that can be is well described in Psalm 133 (TLB):

> How wonderful it is, how pleasant, when brothers live in harmony! For harmony is as precious as the fragrant anointing oil that was poured over Aaron's head, and ran down onto his beard, and onto the border of his robe. Harmony is as refreshing as the dew on Mount Hermon, on the mountains of Israel. And God has pronounced this eternal blessing on Jerusalem, even life forevermore.

·················· **IN A CAPSULE** ··················

Four Don'ts

• **Principle 1** •
Don't be touchy.

• **Principle 2** •
Don't be a reactor.

• Principle 3 •
Don't be picky.

• Principle 4 •
Don't be harsh and judging.

Four Dos

• Principle 1 •
Do talk it out.

• Principle 2 •
Do allow other opinions.

• Principle 3 •
Do be more tolerant.

• Principle 4 •
Do stay right with God.

Conclusion

The Glue That Cements People Together

Five love principles to make your relationships bloom

LOVE WILL BRING US TOGETHER—BECAUSE
    It breaks through thick barriers.
    It climbs over unsurmountable walls.
    It builds bridges across chasms.

LOVE WILL BRING US TOGETHER—BECAUSE
    It overlooks faults.
    It forgives and forgets.
    It brings us back together.

LOVE WILL BRING US TOGETHER—BECAUSE
> It tunes in.
>
> It understands.
>
> It gives.

LOVE WILL BRING US TOGETHER—BECAUSE
> It goes the extra mile.
>
> It works hard.
>
> It never gives up.

This describes the kind of love that really makes our lives work. Without it, we cannot have lasting and rewarding relationships. But when love is the glue that brings us and binds us together, the Golden Rule principle works. By providing us with the power to obey and treat others as we would like to be treated, God's love in us paves our way to success in every level of our lives with others.

Eliminate love, and all the principles we've learned become a body without life and spirit. When all's said and done, love alone adheres us one to another. No wonder 1 Corinthians 13 tells us love is the greatest gift of all!

Love Is Your Greatest Possibility!

Without love, our relationships do not do well or last. When you stop and think about it, you know that from your own experience. Without love, we quickly rub each other the wrong way. Conflict and misunderstanding take the place of communication and understanding. Relationships are torn apart.

The Bible teaches us, "Love does not demand its own way" (1 Cor. 13:5 TLB). God's unselfish pure love is a treasure He not only gives to us but wants to impart within us. By contrast, without God's love within us and working through us, we are selfish. And selfishness rips us apart from others. When it comes to practicing the Golden Rule principle, divine love provides the needed motivation.

The Bible tells us that love is patient and kind, goes the second mile, and looks for the best in the other person. Someone has said, "Love is found by those who can live with human nature as it is." Those who get the most enjoyment out of their relationships have learned to accept the faults in other people and to love them anyway.

A couple of years ago, I spoke at a singles conference in Seattle. While there, I attended one of the workshops and picked up this story, which illustrates very well the superior way of relating to each other out of love.

Somewhere there is a beautiful place called the Land of Warm Fuzzies. The Land of Warm Fuzzies has in the middle of it the most beautiful garden you have ever seen. Flowers of every color, shape, and variety bloom in full beauty. A crystal-clear stream of water flows through the middle of the Land of Warm

Fuzzies, and every kind of tree that you can imagine grows there—towering fir trees, stalwart oaks, beautiful maples, and fruit trees in abundance. The Land of Warm Fuzzies is a paradise.

The people who live in the Land of Warm Fuzzies are happy and healthy. Life excites them. They have no drug or alcohol problems. There are no divorces, child abuse, or emotional illness. When one person has a need, the others respond and take care of it. A close observation of the citizens in the Land of Warm Fuzzies shows that they practice the Golden Rule principle by treating others as they want to be treated. They are always giving others a smile, a warm hug, or a kind word. You might say they are high on love. It seems that they are always giving love away, and as a consequence they are always happy.

Each person who lives in the Land of Warm Fuzzies, whether adult or child, has a well-worn sack over his shoulder. These sacks, which the people carry with them everywhere, are filled with warm fuzzies. And wherever they go, whomever they meet, they give that person a warm fuzzy. That warm fuzzy melts all over the person and makes him feel warm and good from the inside out.

On the other side of the mountain from the Land of Warm Fuzzies lives a wicked old witch. She lives in the Land of the Cold Pricklies. There no one gets along with another person. People stick their tongues out at each other. And they keep their distance from one another.

One day the old witch ventures over the mountain into the Land of Warm Fuzzies, and the warmth and love that she sees there enrage her with jealousy. She decides right there and then she's got to do something to destroy all of this love and happiness. She gives quite a bit of thought to this and comes up with a shameful scheme. She waits under a tree, and soon a young man comes along who, sure enough, has his bag of warm fuzzies over his shoulder. Just as the young man greets her with a smile and reaches in his bag to get a warm fuzzy to give to her, she says, "Stop! You keep giving those warm fuzzies away to everyone you meet, and you're going to run out of warm fuzzies. You had better hold back your warm fuzzies and give them only on special occasions, when someone really needs one."

Deceived by the wicked witch, the young man starts spreading the rumor that if people keep giving their warm fuzzies away they will soon run out.

Soon the happy land becomes a sad land. The warmth turns to coldness. The love turns to rejection and loneliness. Instead of passing out warm fuzzies, people now give each other cold pricklies. A cold prickly is something like an SOS pad. It gives you a scratchy, cold feeling. A cold prickly is a frown, a rejection, an accusation. A cold prickly comes out in words such as "Do it yourself, idiot," or, "Leave me alone." In a marriage, a cold prickly comes out: "You're sleeping on the couch," or, "No warmth for you tonight."

To put this into the language of Christian faith, Jesus Christ has come bringing us warm fuzzies from God the Father. His way of love is the greatest way to live. To receive Jesus Christ as Lord and Savior is to be born into the family of love. To live for Him means giving and practicing this love in relationships with other people. In fact the Bible clearly teaches that the way we love one another proves whether or not we are children of God. Jesus said, "By this shall all men know that ye are my disciples, if ye have love one to another" (John 13:35).

Not only did Jesus teach us to love one another, but He showed us how to love each other. He related to both friends and enemies out of love.

On the last evening He spent with His disciples, Jesus taught them an unforgettable lesson of love. The account begins with these words: "Now before the feast of the Passover, when Jesus knew that his hour was come that he should depart out of this world unto the Father, having loved his own which were in the world, he loved them unto the end" (John 13:1).

The account continues by telling us that He washed and wiped each of His disciple's feet. What was this? It expressed His deep love for each one of the disciples. At His darkest hour, Jesus thought not of Himself but of others.

Jesus, after giving His love, said, "If I then, your Lord and Master, have washed your feet; ye also ought to wash one another's feet. For I have given you an example, that ye should do as I have done to you"

(John 13:14, 15). Jesus is our example of how to relate to each other in love and service.

When you lie in a casket, your life on this earth ended, what will the people who attend your funeral service be thinking? What will they remember about you? They probably won't care too much whether or not you got the washing and ironing done or whether you got the remodeling finished. Neither will they feel deeply about those things that you have toiled so hard for. But they will remember with feeling whether or not you related to them out of love.

Love is one gift you can afford to give to everyone, beginning with those closest to you. If you do give love, when you die you will hear the words of our Lord, "Well done, thou good and faithful servant. Enter into the joys of the Lord." And those who have known you will miss you, because they will love you.

When it comes to getting along, love is your greatest possibility! So practice this number-one love principle:

• Principle 1 •

Make love your top priority.

One of my dear friends, Mrs. Peterson, who is a youthful senior citizen, sent me a story about the baseball great Willie Stargill, who was a major league baseball star for twenty-one seasons. In the article Willie tells how in September of his last season he was deeply touched by the response of the fans. As Stargill went from ballpark to ballpark to play for the last time, most teams held a special ceremony for him, and the fans gave him a tremendous showing of appreciation. The famous baseball star related, "Tears often streamed out of my eyes when the crowd gave me my final ovation. It seems that in every city they were beautiful in their own way, but none was as appealing as the one after my return from our last West Coast trip. I ran like a kid to my car, for I knew my children were staying up to greet me. It was 3:30 AM; I was gearing for a party. There's nothing that I would rather be than a good father, a dream that means more to me than anything that I have ever accomplished in baseball."

Wasn't that beautiful? I'd say here is a man who has his priorities straight.

Someone has said, "What is success if, when you're standing at the top, having achieved everything you wanted to achieve, you have no one to share it with?" Make love your number-one aim! Love is your greatest possibility in the one life you have to live.

Love Is Your Best Choice!

As you and I live out our everyday relationships, we face many choices. Perhaps the greatest of these is the decision to love or not to love. It faces us frequently and is most important to our inner peace and attitudes toward others. Whether it concerns our inner, middle, or outer circle, we reap the results of our choice between loving and not loving. It is your decision; no one will make it for you. Love is always your best alternative.

Always Act in Love

The second love principle you need to know is this one:

• **Principle 2** •

*Love is something you do because
it is the right thing to do.*

The Lord Jesus commands us to choose love in these words: "A new commandment I give unto you, That ye love one another; as I have loved you, that ye also love one another" (John 13:34). For the Christian, love is the only choice.

So often we try to substitute all kinds of other things to keep from doing what we know is right. But no relationships can turn out well until we do what's right and put love into practice.

Love Is Something You Do, Regardless of How You Feel. You can't afford to allow changing feelings to run your life. If you only treat people well when you feel good, you're robbing yourself and shortchanging the people around you. Do not live primarily by your emotions, but by the teachings of Jesus Christ.

One verse that has been going through my mind again and again in recent days is this: "Having loved his own which were in the world, he loved them unto the end" (John 13:1). Jesus had made the commitment to love. As I have studied the events leading up to the crucifixion of Jesus, I see that Jesus Christ had an undying commitment to loving *anyway*. He did not let mistreatment, betrayal, difficult behavior, or anything else stop Him from choosing to put love into practice. He perfectly exemplifies how we are to put love into practice in all our relationships, no matter how we feel.

In John 20:24–29 we read of the Resurrection appearance of Jesus to Thomas. Not being there at Jesus' first appearance to the disciples, Thomas refused to believe Jesus was risen. This skeptic said, "I won't believe unless I can put my fingers in His side." Thomas would have worn out most people's patience. He was always the last one to accept anything. He tended to look on the dark side and be melancholy.

How patient and loving Jesus was with Thomas. He called him by his name, "Thomas!" He invited him to come and place his fingers in the nail prints and thrust his hand in His side. At that moment Jesus' attitude toward Thomas paid off. Because His love finally all came alive inside Thomas when he experienced it for himself and said, "My Lord and my God" (John 20:28).

Nothing will make this kind of love come alive in you like a personal encounter with the risen Lord

Jesus. To know Him is to love Him, and to love Him is to love others.

Love Is Something You Do, No Matter What Others Do. Our relationships slide downhill fast whenever we surrender leadership to negative feelings and allow those feelings to restrain us from taking right actions.

Back in 1976, before building our own church facilities, we rented a small church building no longer used by the denomination that owned it. We had enjoyed the use of all the facilities for about a year when one day a newly appointed missionary pastor of the denomination came by. He informed us that he was starting a new church in a nearby area and would be taking a lot of the furnishings. Well, when you get used to having something, it's hard to see it taken away from you. I admit I was having some rather resentful feelings about all this. In the days that followed, as the pastor kept coming with a truck and taking more and more furnishings out from under us, it didn't help my feelings any.

Who does he think he is, taking our desk, file cabinet, bookshelves, tables, and all these things we've been using? I thought. Then he informed us he was going to come and take the chairs. I got uptight and resentful.

Finally I decided, *This is ridiculous. Rather than surrender the leadership of my life to these negative emotions, I am going to make the choice to do what is right.*

The next day, when he came to get the chairs, I stopped what I was doing and helped him load them. I wished him the best of everything in his new ministry. And as he drove off, I felt a peaceful joy and love inside. Negative emotions had been overcome with turned-on love in action.

Respond Out of Love, Not Fear

In our relationships we continually make the choice to relate either out of love or fear. Unfortunately the majority of people live below the abundant-life plane and mostly relate out of fear. The Bible teaches that as we live in fellowship with Christ and grow in God's love, fear is cast out of our lives and love becomes the dominant characteristic of the way we relate (see 1 John 4:18).

Have you discovered how fully, completely, and unconditionally you are loved by Father God? You need not earn love, because you are loved. Once you accept and realize this, it gives you a great security. You have the assurance that you are His child, the Spirit of God bearing witness to that within your spirit (see 1 John 4:13; Rom. 8:16). What an experience! His love frees us to lovingly relate to others. The Bible says, "For God hath not given us the spirit of fear; but of power, and of love, and of a sound mind" (2 Tim. 1:7). Choose to practice this third love principle:

• Principle 3 •

Choose to relate to others out of love, not out of fear.

Ask yourself: How do I relate to people?

At a weekly training session with our church's lay leaders, a public-school teacher present said that the children in her classroom who are deeply entrenched in fear cannot even learn. With a warm smile, she went on to say that love alone healed them and brought them out of the pits of fear. It's true, love works a miracle. And it can work the miracle that you need in your life and your relationships.

A great example of one who related out of love instead of out of fear was Father Damien, a courageous Roman Catholic missionary who, from 1873 to 1889, worked for God in a leper colony. The colony was located on the Hawaiian Island of Molokai.

A recent television program told the story, beginning with Father Damien's arrival by ship. Before the missionary got off the ship, the captain, with a scornful laugh, told him he wouldn't stay long in the leper colony but, like all the other clergymen, would return soon to the ship.

As the priest prepared to step from the large ship to a small rowboat that would take him ashore, the leper at the oars held out his hand to help the priest into the boat. Seized by the fear of leprosy, the priest refused the man's hand. Hurt and separation showed in the leper's eyes as he held out the oar for the priest to grasp.

Arriving at the colony, Father Damien found his church building in shambles and his congregation nonexistent. The lepers wanted nothing to do with him and his touch-me-not brand of Christianity. The priest beat on the bell to summon people to the church, but the lepers turned deaf ears to all his pleas and calls.

Beaten and giving up, Father Damien made his way back to the ship, which had returned to the colony. On board, however, something happened that changed his life and was to literally transform the leper colony.

A load of lumber intended for another Catholic parish was on board. Seeing it, the priest demanded that the captain drop the lumber off here for the lepers. The captain refused.

Also on board was a fresh band of untouchable lepers to be dropped at the colony. Father Damien, caught up in a cause greater than himself, forgot about his fear and, in love, picked up a little girl who had leprosy. Holding her close, he gently kissed her little cheek. Then he threatened the captain that unless he lowered the lumber and left it for the leper colony, the little girl would kiss him. The fearful captain immediately agreed to the priest's demand.

Word spread quickly that the priest had touched the little girl with leprosy. By the time Father Damien arrived back in the colony with the load of lumber and the new band of lepers, the colony's citizens had gathered excitedly to see what was happening.

Father Damien announced that instead of using the lumber to build the church first, they would together build a hospital to care for the needs of the people. Isn't that what a church is supposed to be anyway—a hospital to care for the needs of the hurting, the wounded, and the broken?

In the story you see the transforming miracle of love. As Father Damien reached out and touched the untouchable, love came alive, and love worked the miracle. Estranged, suffering, lonely people drew together in a serving, caring, healing love for one another.

Love is the greatest communication there is! And God wants to use your life to:

> Speak the words of love.
> Reach out and touch someone in love.
> Give His love to someone who, this Day,
> feels anything but loved.

Love Given Away Enhances and Enriches All Relationships

My senior-citizen mother, who has been a tremendous boost and blessing in my life, gave me this poem that she'd saved for me along with some other collected treasures. As you read it, you will get the feeling of how every human being, regardless of age, has a deep need to be touched in love.

Minnie Remembers

God,
my hands are old.
I've never said that out loud before
but they are.
I was so proud of them once.
They were soft
like the velvet smoothness of a firm, ripe
    peach.
Now the softness is more like worn-out
    sheets or withered leaves.
When did these slender, graceful hands
    become gnarled, shrunken claws?
When, God?
They lie here in my lap,
naked reminders of this worn-out body that
    has served me too well.

How long has it been since someone
    touched me?
Twenty years?
Twenty years I've been a widow
Respected.
Smiled at.
But never touched.
Never held so close that loneliness was
    blotted out.

I remember how my mother used to hold
    me,
God.
When I was hurt in spirit or flesh,
she would gather me close,

202

stroke my silky hair,
and caress my back with her warm hands.
O God, I'm so lonely!

I remember the first boy who ever kissed me.
We were both so new at that!
The taste of young lips and popcorn,
the feeling inside of mysteries to come.
I remember Hank and the babies.
How else can I remember them but together?
Out of the fumbling, awkward attempts of
    new lovers came the babies.
And as they grew, so did our love.
And, God, Hank didn't seem to mind if my
    body thickened and faded a little.
He still loved it.
And touched it.
And we didn't mind if were no longer
    beautiful.
And it felt so good.
And the children hugged me a lot.
O God, I'm lonely!

God, why didn't we raise the kids to be silly
and affectionate as well as
dignified and proper?
You see, they do their duty.
They drive up in their fine cars;
they come to me to pay their respects.
They chatter brightly and reminisce.
But they don't touch me.

They call me "Mom" or "Mother"
or "Grandma."

Never Minnie.
My mother called me Minnie.
So did my friends.
Hank called me Minnie, too.
But they're gone.
And so is Minnie.
Only Grandma is here.
And God! She's lonely!

Donna Swanson[1]

Much of the illness and loneliness in our society is caused by people being starved for someone to touch them with love.

Did you know that the skin on your body has more than half a million nerve endings that send messages to the brain? When you are touched in a healthy, loving way, the message goes to your brain that you are loved and a worthwhile person. But when you get no warm fuzzies, when all you get are cold pricklies as from hugging an SOS pad, your nerve endings send a message to your brain that you are an unloved and unimportant person.

Jesus touched others in love. As you follow Him throughout His ministry, you see Him touching again and again. He "stretched out his hand and touched" the leper, for instance (see Matt. 8:3). When Peter's mother-in-law was sick, Jesus "touched her hand, and the fever left her" (Matt. 8:15). And then there were

1. Donna Swanson, *Mind Song* (Nashville: Upper Room, 1978). Used by permission.

the little children: "And he took them up in his arms, put his hands upon them, and blessed them" (Mark 10:16). Jesus was a compassionate toucher.

Spokesmen for medical science now say that hugging is a miracle medicine capable of relieving many physical and emotional problems. Dr. David Bressler, director of the Pain Control Unit at UCLA, says, "The type of hugging I recommend is the big bear hug. Use both arms, face your partner, and perform a full embrace. I often tell my patients to use hugging as a part of their treatment for pain. To be held is enormously therapeutic."

Researchers have discovered that hugging can help you live longer, protect you against illness, cure depression and stress, strengthen family relationships, and even help you sleep without pills. Dr. Bressler says, "Hug your spouse, your children, close friends, relatives. If you live alone, the warm embrace with a friend whenever you meet is just as beneficial. It's a marvelous way to improve the quality of your life."

Dr. Bressler says he often writes out for his patients such prescriptions as "Four hugs a day—one at breakfast, at lunch, at dinner, and at bedtime." To improve the quality of your life with others, practice this fourth love principle:

• **Principle 4** •
Reach out and give the touch of love.

Parents, one of the best things you can do in your home is to put your child on your lap and give him a hug. Husband, when you walk into the house after work, give your wife an affectionate hug. Do you want to know how you can communicate love in your family? Kiss everyone good night. Scores of families are hurting simply because they go for days and weeks and months without touching each other in healthy, happy love. The touch of love when given out of a heart of love can draw us together like nothing else.

Treat Others with Love

I shall never forget conducting one of my first funerals as a young minister. Three people in a family had been killed in an accident. Those left behind were grief stricken. I didn't know what to say, so I just went and sat with the family members. I put my arms around each and told them that I loved them. Later these people told me that this gesture touched and helped them more than anything I could have said or done.

The fifth and last principle of this book is one that I hope you will never forget as long as you live.

• Principle 5 •

Love people, and they will love you back.

Love is the greatest, and love works wonders. People always know when you love them and when you don't. They usually respond in the same way as they are treated. Treat others with love, and they will respond with love. Withhold your love, and they, too, will withhold their love.

I now close with a word of prayer for you and with a lesson I learned from children.

My prayer for you:

May you feel so loved by Father God, so secure, so complete, so enriched, so favored, and so accepted, that you will be set free to reach out in love and treat others as you want to be treated. May the timeless principles for getting along continue to live on in you. And as these are put into practice, may they cause your relationships to bloom and increase in beauty with the passing years.

May this book cause you to become a lifetime student of human relationships, because when it comes to understanding other people and getting along, there is no end to the fascinating learning process. Last, may this book not be an ending but only a beginning of learning and working at building love with the people in your life.

Some children taught me a simple yet profound lesson one Sunday when I was pastoring my first church, in Columbus, Ohio. As I stepped in to observe, I saw the happy faces of those four- and five-year-olds as they sang in their high-pitched little voices:

Love is something, if you give it away, give
   it away.
It's just like a magic penny,
If you give it away, you end up having more.

························ **IN A CAPSULE** ························

• Principle 1 •

Make love your top priority.

• Principle 2 •

*Love is something you do because
it is the right thing to do.*

• Principle 3 •

Choose to relate to others out of love, not out of fear.

• Principle 4 •

Reach out and give the touch of love.

• Principle 5 •

Love people, and they will love you back.